Practical *A*
Techniques for
ISO/TS-16949

Practical Auditing Techniques for ISO/TS-16949

Forty years experience of
Raymond J. Ness

Writers Club Press
New York Lincoln Shanghai

Practical Auditing Techniques for ISO/TS-16949

Writers Club Press
an imprint of iUniverse, Inc.

For information address:
iUniverse, Inc.
2021 Pine Lake Road, Suite 100
Lincoln, NE 68512
www.iuniverse.com

Author's Contact Information:
5072 Wembley Ct.
Wyoming, MI 49509
616-534-9176

ISBN: 0-595-27312-2

Printed in the United States of America

Contents

I.
Prologue

The purpose of this book is to present a method of pragmatic auditing that an auditor may use to perform an internal or external audit. The book will follow the standard of ISO/TS-16949:1999 through all of the process/functions. The limitations, as viewed by the author, are that this is only one method that may be employed. It is not the definitive method for auditing. This is a method that may be modified or changed by anyone. It is the hope of the author that readers of this book will change the method or adopt a new method to further the auditing process. This process is a vital feedback to the auditee in order to improve the process of producing parts or service to the customer. There have been too many instances where the auditee believes that the auditing process is a punitive one. This is definitely not the case. The audit process is an objective learning process where the auditee knows of the strengths and weaknesses of the quality management system. The corrective actions that are performed are in themselves a learning process in solving problems. A combined joint effort is to be employed in order to achieve success in establishing, monitoring, and implementing this system.

The scope will follow the specification through all of the functions of a common business. The examples are slanted to a manufacturing process for the automotive industry, but this book and its methods can be applied to any business. A reference is made to functions or processes. A process is a series of activities that produce a product as its output. Inputs of all sorts are transformed through a process to an output. All endeavors are to a process and there are certain functions that carry out these processes to produce the prescribed product. The scope of this audit process encompasses a holistic approach of all processes/functions working together. In this way, the auditor will cover all of the requirements through a smooth flow in a way a business naturally operates.

The assumptions of the author are that the reader(s) are versed in QS-9000 or at the least ISO-9000. Those of you that are not, will find some difficulty in the book. However, there is value in the content for you that are contemplating being registered to a standard. Those that are not desiring to be registered will also find a valued use in preparing systems for their own mission statement

There are certain acronyms and words that strictly related to the automotive industry. However, if the author cannot convey the ideas in a lucid manner, then the reader will not flourish. To paraphrase an old philosopher, the shadows of the cave are to illuminate to reveal actual reality. The actual reality is the truth. The objective of this book is to enlighten, inform, and educate. If this is accomplished, then the author is satisfied. It is encouraged that the readers of this book contact the author with corrections, additions, or suggestions.

II.
Review and Audit of the Documents

There are many phases to the auditing process, depending upon which reference is consulted. Typically there will be between three to six phases. The ISO/TS-16949 standard uses an attachment I to describe the rules for certification. This is officially known as the Automotive certification scheme for ISO/TS-16949, Rules for achieving IATF recognition, Second edition. This attachment describes five (5) phases to the audit process that are: activities before the audit; audit planning; site audit and reports; nonconformity's management; certification issue. This chapter will cover the Activities before the audit. It is recommended that anyone attempting the certification process obtain this attachment.

There are 13 essential items required before the audit. These are enumerated in the attachment. They are as follows:

1. Number of employees in the organization. This would include all employees both in manufacturing and the office. If there are multiple sites, then all of the sites including the support sites should be listed. Support sites are defined as sales, engineering, purchasing, and information services. These sites support the manufacturing sites in functions that are not located at the manufacturing sites. All of these support sites will have to be audited in order to fulfill the requirements of ISO/TS-16949. This is also covered in attachment I. There is a chart for the number of audit days required for the audit. It is based on the number of employees as was the case for ISO and QS 9000. As a side note, it is helpful to the auditor to know which sites support the manufacturing site (s). An aid to the auditor is a matrix chart showing all of the sites and the primary and secondary responsibilities for all of the typical functions. This matrix is of great help to the first audit and the ensuing surveillance audits. It clearly describes where the functions are located at the sites.

Site/Fn.	Mgt.	Sales	Mfg.	Q.A.	Eng.	Lab	Purch.
Corp.	Yes	Yes	No	No	Yes	Yes	No
Plant A	Yes	No	Yes	Yes	Yes	Yes	Yes
Plant B	Yes	No	Yes	Yes	No	Yes	No
Plant C	Yes	No	Yes	Yes	No	Yes	Yes

2. A description of the products and services made.

A short description of all of the products and/or services is needed to help in developing the scope of the audit. This description will also help the auditor in determining the audit plan and who will be qualified to perform the audit. Annex 2 of attachment 1 lists the requirements for auditors. There should be at least one of the auditors with the required experience related to the auditee's product line. An additional description, though not necessary, would be a listing of the processes used to manufacture the above mentioned products. A floor plan of the facility (facilities if there are more than one) is another helpful aid. These descriptions will help the auditor to understand the processes as much as possible the entire focus of the organization of the auditee. Planning the audit will be enhanced by the submission of this information.

3. Operational Performance Trends for the Previous Twelve(12) months, minimum. If the auditee is QS-9000 registered, then this is analogous to the sub element 4.1.5 of QS-9000. This is the "Analysis and uses of Company Level Data". This, if the auditee is a FORD supplier, is the QOS data. This will also be the customer performance reports from all customers, if they are provided. This information will be reviewed by the auditor as to the direction of the trends. A typical question arises as to how is the present system dealing with the auditee's customers both internal and external. Late in this review process, the auditor will make a decision if the auditee is ready to be audited. If the trends reveal a favorable outlook, then the next stage will commence. If the data show unfavorable trends, then the audit may be postponed until these trends have been improved. The final objective is to achieve success with this system in view of the standard. To perform the audit prematurely, would only cause the auditee work that is not value added. This would also be the case if there was not a sufficient amount of data. Too little data may be a symptom of a system that has not had enough time to mature. There must be substantive evidence to audit in order to determine if the system is effective. A rule of thumb, although not always necessary, would be to have about three months of data to present for the auditor. Of course if the

auditee is already QS-9000, then the amount of data would only pertain to the new items in ISO/TS-16949.

4. Scope of the Certification. This will encompass the depth and breadth of the certification. The entirety of the audit process will be directed at the scope. The scope will be listed on the certification document. The scope is what is accomplished at the site or sites. An example of a scope would be "Design and manufacture of precision metal stampings for the automotive and office furniture industry". Within the scope there must be the complete listing of all of the sites. The certificate will list all of the manufacturing sites as well as the support sites. These support sites will include sales offices, design engineering offices, or any outside services that support the manufacturing site(s). The auditee does have the choice to not include sites. However, if these sites subsequently are found to support the manufacturing or any other sites, then these sites will have to be audited. This will cause a delay to the audit process. There is a time limit to the fulfillment of the audit process. The time limit is to complete the audit process is 90 days from the end of the on-site audit. All corrective actions must be completed within this time frame. This also includes any nonconformance in the document review as well.

5. Product Design Responsibility. The definition of product design responsibility is given in Annex A of the standard (A18). Suppliers with authority to establish a new, or change an existing product specification for product delivered to a customer. A note in the definition, used for guidance, states that this responsibility includes testing and verification of design performance. This is the same definition that was given for suppliers in QS-9000. Again, approval by the customer does not waive the supplier's design responsibility status. It is up to the auditee to describe the status of this responsibility to the auditor. This status could be split between various customers. A supplier could be design responsible to General Motors but not to Toyota or Honda. If the design is shared with an outside source, then this relationship must be described to the auditor. The auditor must verify that the supplier(auditee) and any outside subcontracted design have the capability to comply with element 4.4. If it is required, the auditor will audit these subcontractors for compliance to fulfill the audit process. The auditee should be prepared for this type of audit and prepare the subcontracted sources.

6. Sites to be registered. A site is defined(A.54) as a location where value added production processes occur. Much of this discussion was covered in Scope of the Certification.

7. Remote locations. A remote location is defined(A.52) as a location that supports sites and at which non-production processes occur. These are Engineer-

ing centers, Sales, or Purchasing that may be part of an overall corporate scheme. Again this was discussed in the Scope of the Certification previously.

8. Quality systems certifications obtained. This section should be fairly obvious to those who have obtained recognition. It is of importance to the auditor as to what recognition achievements have been obtained. ISO/TS-16949 when coupled with customer requirements, is the equivalent to QS-9000. This is according to FORD MOTOR CO. The auditor will be prepared to look for QOS measurements if the auditee has a Q-1 award. In addition, if there has been recognition by other automotive suppliers, then these should be included as well. As will be discussed later, the auditee will provide all customer specifics to the auditor.

9. Quality manual. This is the level 1 manual of the organization's policies. It is strongly recommended that the level 2 documents be submitted also. The level 2 documents are the procedures that support the policies. Later we will discuss how the document review is performed to verify compliance to the standard.

10. Internal audit and management review planning and results from previous twelve (12) months. If the auditee is ISO or QS-9000 certified, then this is not a problem. The purpose of this information is for the auditor to view what has been discussed during these reviews. In some cases, if there are concerns that have not been resolved in a timely manner, then the auditor will concentrate on those concerns. This is a more value added audit. Another purpose would be to check the retention time of these records to the section in the standard or to the documented times from the quality manual. One important point to remember is that the internal audit is to be performed to the ISO/TS-16949 standard. If the latest internal audits only show ISO or QS requirements, then the auditor will write a Major nonconformance. This is because the auditee has not implemented the internal audit element.

11. List of qualified internal auditors. During the on-site audit the auditor will use this list to verify independence of the auditors in their respective areas. When in the Human Resources or Training department, the auditor will ask to see the training records of these individuals. It is important to note that certain customers will have requirements for the auditee's internal auditors. General Motors requires that the internal auditors comply with ISO-10011-2-1994. This requires the internal auditors to have at least a secondary education, training in the standard(s), competence through written or oral examinations, two years experience in quality assurance activities, and participated in four audits. This is only a partial listing of all of that is required. The auditee should inquire to their customers to reveal what are the requirements, if any.

12. List of customer and customer specific requirements. This information is probably the most important next to the customer performance reports. The list of customers is everyone that the auditee has a contract to ship product. This is can easily be obtained from the Sales/Marketing function. The latter part, customer specific requirements, is not so easy to obtain. Customer specifics, as mentioned before, coupled with the standard is the equivalent to QS-9000. These specifics should tell the auditee about the Product approval process. This is covered in the standard, ISO/TS-16949, as sub element 4.2.4.11. The sub element states "The supplier shall comply with a product and process approval procedure recognized by the customer". This phrase is used throughout the standard. It is the responsibility of the auditee to know what are these requirements. As was noted in number 11, above, the requirement for internal auditors from General Motors is stated in ISO-10011-2. General Motors also specifies other requirements for compliance to the standard. These requirements are listed on their Internet web site. However, there are other requirements from the European manufacturers. The Italians ANFIA is the equivalent to the North American AIAG. It lists requirements compatible to the FMEA, SPC, and PPAP manuals. They also list requirements for continuous improvement and design of experiments. The French FIEV list requirements for trace ability, process audits, and performance measures. The Germans VDA have documented nine VDA specifics from quality evidence to exhaust emissions. Tier 1 suppliers, those who supply direct to assembly plants, also have requirements of their subcontractors. Organizations such as TRW and Lear have specifics for product submission, control of special product characteristics, and trace ability. These specifics are to be communicated to the auditor in order to complete a full audit to these specifics and the standard.

13. Customer complaints management. This is a list of all customer complaints. The list should extend to the last twelve(12) months. This gives the auditor a better time horizon to view. The list should describe the status of these complaints. Open items will be investigated. There should be a reasonable explanation as to why these have not been closed in a timely manner. The quantity and the status of the complaints should be noted in the management review record. This is a part of customer satisfaction and a measurable in the use of company level data. Included within these complaints should be those to the delivery of 100% to all customers. Sub element 4.15.6.2 of the standard requires corrective action to "...Meet customer and service requirements." These corrective actions listed will be compared to those on the customer's performance reports.

The auditor will review all of the above information to determine if the auditee is prepared for the on-site audit. Again, the goal is to have success with the audit process. Time, labor, and money could be spent because the auditee was not prepared. There is a joint relationship between the auditee and auditor to work together to achieve this success. If is determined that the auditee is not prepared, then the audit can be postponed or a preaudit can be performed. A preaudit is a non binding audit where the auditee is not bound to perform corrective action and the auditor does not provide a report or the audit findings. There is an allowance for one (1) pre-assessment. In most cases for pre-assessments the auditee does implement corrective on their own and the auditor does provide a variation of a draft report in the form of noncompliance's. To reiterate, this process has a time limit of 90 days. If the auditee is not prepared by the determination of the auditor reviewing the submitted data, then it is the obligation of the auditor to promptly inform the auditee of this fact.

The actual documentation audit involves the level 1 and 2 documents. The level is the Quality manual also known as the policy manual, and the level 2, procedures. These documents were mentioned in the above paragraph no.9. This audit of the documentation is one of the most important audits to be done. The foundation of the entire system is based on the policies and procedures formulated by the auditee. The auditor will compare what is in the standard to what are submitted and make a ruling as to the conformance or nonconformance of what is written. There are occurrences when the documentation submitted is not exactly enumerated in the same manner as the standard. There is nothing wrong with an alternative scheme for the quality and/or procedure manual. However, if the auditor cannot locate the specific element or sub element, then a nonconformance will be written due to lack of direction or guidance. In this light of understanding, a recommendation is noted for the auditee to aid the auditor in correctly locating the proper elements. A tabulation is created identifying all of the elements and a reference location on the manual(s). The following is an example:

ISO/TS-16049	Quality Manual	Quality Procedure
4.1.1.1	1.1.1.A	QSP-100
4.1.1.2	1.1.2 B	QSP-100
4.2.4.1	2.4.1	QSP-204
4.2.4.10	2.4.10 K	QSP-210
4.4.2.1	4.2.1 B	QSP-425

4.6.1.2	6.2.1 J	QSP-600
4.10.2.1	10.2.1 E	QSP-1000

For an example, if the auditor is searching for the requirements to sub element 4.2.4.10, control plan, the Quality Manual reference is 2.4.10 K and the procedure is QSP-210. The use of a table such as the above is also valuable for internal audits. New auditors can facilitate the ease of the audit by using the table in a step-by-step approach.

With the use of the table and the documents, the auditor reads the standard element or sub element. Then the document, level 1 Quality Manual, is read. There is a comparison to detect whether the manual reference conforms to the standard. All "SHALLs" are to be addressed in the documentation. If the required "SHALL" have not been met in manual, then the auditor will look for it in the procedure. In the event that neither source can answer the requirement, a nonconformance is written. This method continues until the entire documentation is complete. This method is simple, straightforward, and basic for anyone to perform. It is highly recommended that all auditees perform this audit before submitting their documents to the auditor. This could save a lot of time and extra work.

Writing the nonconformance to the documentation should be an exercise in learning for the auditor and auditee. The auditor has the obligation to inform the auditee of the deviation from the norm. Additionally, the auditor cannot tell the auditee how to correct the nonconformance. The two constraints lead the auditor to writing the nonconformance in a value added manner. This can be done by the use of the interrogative method. A formulation of a question to prompt the auditee to search for the answer within the documentation or the standard is in order. For example if there was no mention of having contract review records, the nonconformance might say "Do you retain contract review records, and are they retained in element 4.16?" This then sends a signal to the auditee that the records need to be included in the element 4.3 and to look in element 4.16 to determine the retention time period. The absence of direct quotes from the standard may require the auditor to look further into the intention of the auditee. The implicit wording of the sections of the manual will require the auditor to read more intently to judge whether there is compliance. A guide to this judgment is to err on the side of being conservative. If the particular wording is vague as to answering the requirements, then a noncompliance should be written. The noncompliance would state that it is unclear how this complies to the standard. If the auditee disagrees with this judgment, the auditor should ask for clarification in order to better understand the intent. Remember, this is a learning and discovery process for both parties. The objective is to gain understanding of both views.

A final note to help both auditee and auditor is the judicious marking of the standard. It is a helpful aid to mark the important words in the standard. The much used method is the use of hi-lite markers of three colors. The important words are the "SHALLs", "PROCEDUREs", and "RECORDs" in the standard. The purpose for marking is to locate these words for easy access when performing an audit. It is a valid question by the auditee to the auditor to ask where in the standard is it required to have these shalls, procedures, and records. The auditor must demonstrate knowledge of the standard by explaining to the auditee where these important requirements are located. It is a helpful aid to have these words identified and a professional manner to find them quickly. This is a learning process and part of the learning is demonstration of knowledge of the standard.

The documentation of the Quality system is to be created judiciously with the intent of satisfying the standard or specification and the requirements of the auditee. There have been too many times when unnecessary procedures and/or work instructions have been written to satisfy a consultant or a PRE-written documentation program. In most of these there have been nonconformances written due to the lack of implementing these "needed" documents. The standard requires a certain amount of required procedures and work instructions. The auditee should create the minimum that is needed, then through an internal or external audit(s) make a further determination if such documentation is necessary. The key idea, as stated before, is that this is an objective learning experience.

III.

Planning the On-site Audit

Planning the on-site audit requires the gathering of information for the preparation. The required information consists of the number of employees, number of buildings and locations, number of shifts and the times, name of the management representative, scope of the audit, and the standard to be audited. Additional information is the qualification of the auditors, number of auditors, and language capability. Attachment I of the certification scheme describe in annex 3 the quantity of time in man days relevant to the number of employees. Annex 2 is the Criteria for third party auditor qualification. These will be covered later in this chapter as a plan is developed. The auditor shall prepare an audit plan detailing all of the activities and elements to be audited within the scope of the standard and the auditee. All shifts shall be audited and shown on the audit plan. In accordance with ISO-10011-1, sub element 5.2.1, the plan should also include objectives, scope, reference documents, team members, auditee's members, date, location, a schedule of the meetings(opening, debriefings, and closing) and activities(functions) to be audited, auditor assignments, safety and/or regulatory standards, and the report distribution. Preceding the plan, two or three weeks before the audit date, there may be a notice asking for certain reference documents to be prepared at the beginning of the audit. These documents are sometimes known as working papers. These "working papers" could consist of items such as customer performance reports, organizational chart, facility plan, employee list, master list of documents, control plans, drawing and/or specification master list, new projects or products, and product safety standards. The documents are used to facilitate the auditor(s) in the performing the audit.

The criterion for auditors is covered in Annex 2 of Attachment I, Rules for certification bodies. The criterion is more detailed than ISO-10010-2. The Lead Auditor selects any other auditors according to this criteria. In addition, the auditors must have sector relevant experience for the commodity code that is being audited. What this means is that the auditors should have experience in the industry business that is within the auditee's scope. The acceptance criterion for education is a secondary (high school) or university degree. Work experience for new auditors is 3 years of experience in the automotive industry including 2 years in Quality Assurance. Also the auditor must have 8 first or second party audits in the last 3 years. Experienced auditors are to have 15 third party audits in automotive within the last 3 years. Two(2) of these audits have to be as the lead auditor.

Qualification and training for auditors is defined as that the auditor be qualified to ISO-10011-2 and training sponsored by the IATF. The IATF is the International Automotive Task Force. The training consists of practical, written, and oral examinations. The qualified certificate is for three(3) years. This training is sanctioned by the IATF. It is highly recommended that the auditee obtain these documents to fully understand the qualifications of the auditor. It is also recommended that the auditee ask to see the auditor's credentials before the audit.

As was noted previously, Annex 3 of Attachment I have a schedule chart for the amount of time in man days based on the employee level at the site. For our purposes the assumption will be made that the audit will be made for a company with 175 employees. The company is design responsible and does not have any external support sites. All functions are contained in the one site. The initial certification audit will be for eight(8) man days with two(2) auditors. This is a total of 64 hours of auditing not including breaks or lunch. Each man day will consist of eight hours of auditing with debriefing sessions at the end of each day. Lunch will be on-site and is a working lunch to inform the auditee of the status of the audit. The working lunch also is for the auditors to be informed of issues that have arisen. In short, the auditee and the auditors will have two(2) debriefing sessions each day of the audit. The audit will be of a duration of four(4) days. It is essential and professional that the auditor keep the auditee and the auditee's management informed as to the status of the audit. All communication is to be through the Lead auditor and the Management representative. This requirement is to be communicated to the auditee at each audit. It is essential that all communication proceed between the management and the lead auditor.

There are considerations for multi-site corporate schemes. This is described in Attachment I, Annex 3. This will not be discussed here. It is sufficient to say that there is an adjustment for the number of sites and that the certification body must establish how this corporate scheme is to be implemented. This is to be handled through the quotation process.

The audit plan will cover all activities or functions. As in QS-9000, each audit will cover customer complaints, internal audit, continuous improvement, and management review. The plan should be communicated to the auditee well in advance of the scheduled day(s) of the audit. There are proponents that do not agree that all of the items should be conveyed to the auditee before the audit. Yielding to ISO-10011-1, this is not harmful if the disclosure does not compromise the audit. There are situations where the advance notice of the plan serves to update the system of the auditee if only by the communication that the audit is to take place. In the long view, this communication serves to help the auditee and accomplishes the objective of the audit.

The plan covers all functions and activities of the auditee. It describes the various functions to be audited, the time for auditing, and the person who is performing the audit. It is the responsibility of the auditee to provide personnel for the audit and documented of compliance. If key personnel are not present for the audit, the auditee provides back-up personnel. All documented evidence of compliance should be readily available for the auditor.

A typical plan for an audit of 8 man-days with 2 auditors is as follows:

DAY ONE	AUDITOR A	AUDITOR B
8:00 A.M.	Opening	Meeting
	Management	Manufacturing (1st)
9:00	Management	Manufacturing (1st)
	Management (C.I.)	Manufacturing (1st)
10:00	Sales	Manufacturing (1st)
	Sales	Manufacturing (1st)
11:00	Sales	Manufacturing (1st)
	Sales	Manufacturing (1st)
12:00 P.M.	Lunch and	Debrief
	Lunch and	Debrief
1:00	Manufacturing (1st)	Shipping
	Manufacturing (1st)	Shipping
2:00	Manufacturing (1st)	Receiving
	Human Resources	Receiving Inspection
3:00	Human Resources	Receiving Inspection
	Human Resources	Production Control
4:00	Human Resources	Production Control
	First day Debrief	First day Debrief
5:00		
Day one=8 hours each auditor, 16 hours total.		

DAY TWO	AUDITOR A	AUDITOR B
10:00 A.M.	Purchasing	Maintenance
	Purchasing	Maintenance
11:00	Purchasing	Maintenance
	Purchasing	Maintenance
12:00 P.M.	Lunch and	Debrief
	Lunch and	Debrief
1:00	Purchasing	Maintenance
	Q. A. (customer complaints)	Laboratory/Testing
2:00	Q. A. (customer complaints	Laboratory/Testing
	Q. A. (internal audit)	Laboratory/Testing
3:00	Q. A. (internal audit)	Laboratory/Testing
	Manufacturing (2nd)	Manufacturing (2nd)
4:00	Manufacturing (2nd)	Manufacturing (2nd)
	Manufacturing 2nd)	Manufacturing (2nd)
5:00	Manufacturing (2nd)	Manufacturing (2nd)
	Manufacturing (2nd)	Manufacturing (2nd)
6:00	Manufacturing (2nd)	Manufacturing (2nd)
	Second day Debrief	Second day Debrief
7:00		

Day Two=8 hours each auditor: 32 hours total.

DAY THREE	AUDITOR A	AUDITOR B
5:00 a.m.	Manufacturing (3rd)	Manufacturing (3rd)
	Manufacturing (3rd)	Manufacturing (3rd)
6:00	Manufacturing (3rd)	Manufacturing (3rd)
	Manufacturing (3rd)	Manufacturing (3rd)
7:00	Manufacturing (3rd)	Manufacturing (3rd)
	Manufacturing (3rd)	Manufacturing (3rd)
8:00	Engineering (design)	Tool shop/management
	Engineering (design)	Tool shop/management
9:00	Engineering (design)	Quality (calibration)
	Engineering (design)	Quality (calibration)
10:00	Engineering (design)	Quality (calibration)
	Engineering (design)	Quality (calibration)
11:00	Engineering (design)	Quality (calibration)
	Engineering (design)	Quality (calibration)
12:00 p.m.	Lunch and Debrief	Lunch and Debrief
	Lunch and Debrief	Lunch and Debrief
1:00 p.m.	Engineering (design)	I T/MIS/IS
	Engineering (design)	I T/MIS/IS
2:00	Third day Debrief	Third day Debrief

Day Three 16 hours/each: 48 Hours total

DAY FOUR	AUDITOR A	AUDITOR B
7:00 a.m.	Manufacturing	Manufacturing
	Manufacturing	Manufacturing
8:00	Manufacturing (customer specifics)	Manufacturing (customer specifics)
	Manufacturing (customer specifics)	Manufacturing (customer specifics)
9:00	Manufacturing (customer specifics)	Manufacturing (customer specifics)
	Engineering (prod. realization	Manufacturing
10:00	Engineering (prod. realization	Manufacturing (NC product)
	Engineering (prod. realization	Manufacturing (NC product
11:00	Engineering (prod. realization	Manufacturing (NC product
	Engineering (prod. realization	Manufacturing (NC product
12:00 p.m.	Lunch and debrief	Lunch and debrief
	Lunch and debrief	Lunch and debrief
1:00	Engineering/Q.A.	Manufacturing
	(Product approval process)	Manufacturing
2:00	(Product approval process)	Manufacturing
	Assessor Debrief	Assessor Debrief
3:00	Assessor Debrief	Assessor Debrief
	Closing Meeting	Closing Meeting
4:00	DEPART	DEPART

Day Four 16 hours/each: 64 hours total.

This audit plan is then reviewed by the Lead auditor and/of other auditors who will be on the audit. The plan is then faxed/e-mailed/mailed to the auditee for return input. The auditee should review the plan and reply to the Lead auditor as to its suitability. Plans are flexible and should be changed to accommodate both parties if there are conflicts.

When the plan has final approval the lead auditor meets with other auditors to discuss the plan. It is here the lead auditor makes preliminary assignments to the auditors. Completion of these assignments will be done at opening meeting with the auditee and the auditee's guides. The lead auditor should also discuss travel and lodging accommodations for the audit team. Input from the auditee is very helpful if the auditee obtains a discount with a particular hotel or motel chain. Maps to the auditee's location are important for all of the auditors. Communication is the vital essence for the plan and audit to be carried out successfully.

The start of the on-site audit is the opening meeting. As per ISO-10011-1, there are a number of items to be covered.

- Introductions: The key word is to be brief but to explain the connection to the auditee's business. Start with the auditors in order to set the tone for all of the introductions from the auditee.

- Scope and Purpose of the audit: State the standard that will be audited for compliance and the auditee's documents. It is important to communicate that the audit will be to not only the standard, but to whatever is used as documentation by the auditee.

- Methods: Describe the tactics or methods that will be used during the audit. These are usually direct questions, reading of the documents, and observations. State that there must be objective evidence to show compliance or non-compliance.

- Communication Links: The official communication link is between the Lead Auditor and the Auditee's Management Representative. This means that all communications pass through this link. This is usually performed during the debrief sessions that are scheduled in the audit plan. The auditee may request that there be more frequent communication. The Lead auditor should accommodate as best as possible as long as the request does not interfere with the audit objective.

- Facilities: Ask for a centralized location to conduct the debriefing sessions. In addition, locate the lavatories. Emphasize the important of safety for all in the audit. Request that operators in manufacturing may be allowed to step away from their operations so as not to be injured. Inquire about the safety conditions that the auditors will need. These items could be safety glasses, hard hats, safety shoes, or ear plugs.

- The Plan: Read and describe the plan in detail to all of the attendees at the opening meeting. This serves to clarify the full objective of the audit. Ask if there are any questions about the plan. If there are conflicts, make corrections accordingly. The auditors participating in the audit should be given additional assignments. With the help of the auditee and a facility plan, designate on the facility plan the locations to be audited by the auditors. Ensure that all activities, cells, or lines are covered during the audit. During the debrief sessions, confer with the other auditors as to the status of these designations. Also in the debrief sessions, there should be a status report as to the number of nonconformances and their status. The status of the nonconformances would be whether minor of major.

- Nonconformances and Opportunities for Improvement: Explain the definitions of minor and major nonconformances. Describe that objective evidence is needed to demonstrate conformance of implementation. Nonconformances are written against the standard and the documented system of the auditee. As per Attachment I of the rules of certification, non conformities are recorded even if corrective action is implemented immediately. The nonconformance is to be acknowledged by the auditee. This is usually done by a counter signature on the nonconformance form. This means that that the person signing the form has witnessed the nonconformance. It does not mean that signed person is responsible to correct it or that the person agrees or disagrees. It is a witnessing signature. Opportunities for improvement are items that need to be addressed in order to improve the system. These "suggestions" could be that the manufacturing areas are in need of better housekeeping, or there is too much scrap in the nonconforming area, or the nonconforming material is not disposition in a timely manner. Opportunities for improvement are not non conformities. An auditor does a disservice to the auditee if discrepancies are not noted. The intent is a learning experience, not a deception.

Roles of the Guides: The auditor(s) will need guides to help them access all areas and personnel. The role of the guide is an active one. The guide will have to know almost all aspects of the system and the business. If the auditor feels that the guide is not cooperating or is not knowledgeable, then a replacement will be requested. The guide will act as an interpreter for special language that is used by the auditee's personnel. Keeping the auditor on time is also the responsibility of the guide by following the audit plan. The guide should notify the auditor of the time limits for each sedation or function of the audit. However, the auditor has sole control of the audit. The auditor can expand or contract the various time frames of the audit. The rationale for this action is the availability of the objective evidence for compliance. Additionally, if the auditor is following an audit trail, then the time frame may be extended. The auditor and lead auditor must keep control of the audit. The participation of observers and consultants is kept to that of being silent. These individuals are not to participate in the audit. The auditor reserves the right to halt the audit if there is interference from these individuals.

Debriefing sessions with the auditee and the auditors are held to communicate the status of the audit. The lead auditor should review all nonconformances written by the auditors. Conversely the auditors should review the nonconformances written by the lead auditor. The purpose of this exercise is to ensure uniformity and eliminate duplication of the nonconformances. To retain of exclude the nonconformances is the decision of the lead auditor. The management representative should be apprised of all of these decisions. Attachment I of the rules of certification, allows for the termination of the audit if there is a major nonconformance. This is done in conjunction with a meeting with the lead auditor. The lead auditor should ask the management representative if senior management had been informed of the status of the audit findings. This is a good practice so that there are no surprises at the closing meeting. Heading off these "confrontations" is good professional practice of the audit team. The closing meeting should proceed smoothly to complete the on-site audit process.

The closing meeting is held with the auditee's personnel and all of the auditors present. All of the nonconformances with a summary report should be copied for the auditee's management representative. The management representative may make additional copies as necessary for any of the auditee's personnel. The lead auditor begins the meeting by thanking everyone for their cooperation during the audit. Positive, value added, beneficial items found during the audit are stated to the auditee. These favorable items should be noted in the report also. Opportunities for improvement are also read to acknowledge that there are some areas in need of additional help. The scope of the audit is read to reiterate the original intent of the audit. All of the nonconformances are read aloud. This is done so as to inform all those concerned the status of the entire audit. Questions may arise as to clarification of the nonconformances. These are answered by the auditor who wrote the nonconformance. It is important that the lead auditor convey the auditee's personnel that this a time for clarification of the nonconformances and not for discussion of corrective action. The corrective action is the responsibility of the auditee. Long discussions about how to correct the nonconformances only lead to protracted closing meeting. This is not productive to the informational phase of the audit.

The lead auditor is to communicate to the auditee the requirements for corrective action. The corrective actions are to be completed within 90 days of the on-site audit. The details of the corrective actin is that they follow element 4.14 of the standard. The auditee is to provide the following format as a corrective action: .

- The problem from the noncompliance. This can be the copy of the original nonconformance.

- The root cause of the problem. This is in accordance with sub element 4.14.2.1.b of the standard. This is an investigation of the cause not just a cursory review of what could be the cause.

- The corrective action taken to correct the nonconformance. This is sometimes called the immediate corrective action. The corrective action is to eliminate the cause. This is stated in sub element 4.14.2.1.c of the standard.

- Prevention measures are to used to prevent recurrence. These are controls to ensure that the problem does not occur again. This can be the use of a known procedure presently in the system of the auditee. This is also referenced by 4.14.2.1.d and 4.14.3.c of the standard. This is an important point to review by the auditor when the corrective actions are received. If there are no controls, the problem will occur again.

- Verification of Effectiveness and Evidence are essential to show the reviewing auditor that the corrective action has been implemented. The evidence provided shows that the problem has been corrected. Without evidence, there is no proof that corrections have been done.

Systemic action the corrective action impact to other areas or functions. These could be processes or products within the confines of the audited facility. They can extend beyond the facility if there are remote locations such as engineering or sales. Systemic action is to be the extension of the problem to other areas, functions, departments, or groups. Since the auditors only perform a sampling of the entire system, there could areas that was not observed. No nonconformances in an area or function does not mean tacit approval that everything there is perfect. The auditee should cover all aspects of the nonconformance in every area concerned.

The timing of the corrective actions is to be communicated to the auditee. The requirements for corrective action should be communicated very explicitly to the auditee. This can be accomplished by having a typed form to be handed to the management representative during the closing meeting. The time frame for closure according to attachment I of the rules is 90 days from the end of the site visit. Certificates will be issued only if there is full compliance to all requirements. This means that all corrective actions are to be closed with evidence of closure. The audit team may require an on-site follow up to the corrective actions to verify that they have been closed.

The above paragraphs are a brief overview of the essential workings of an audit and the planning. To experience the audit process in full, one needs to go through the process on a first hand basis.

IV.
Management

After you have conducted your opening meeting, the plan will most likely call for an audit of management. Doing this section early in the audit gains a view of the philosophy for the entire organization. The standard states in 4.1.1.1 that *The supplier's management with executive responsibility shall define and document its policy for quality, including objectives for quality and its commitment to quality.* Who is this person(s) and what is executive responsibility? This person (s) is setting the tone and philosophy for the whole organization. Will you be auditing the correct individual (s)? The standard contains a glossary that defines executive responsibility (A.23)" Responsibility for profit and loss". This person might be the plant manager, president, owner, CEO, or a vice president of operations. In short, there might be a great variety of titles. The key defining factor is that the individual has this responsibility for profit and loss in the organization. Quality managers, although very intelligent and good at their jobs, are not usually responsible for profit and loss. The auditor will need to talk to the person (s) that fit the glossary definition.

Along these lines of inquiry, the auditor should know who is the management representative. The management representative should be clearly defined. This is usually accomplished by way of an organizational chart or a documented item in the policy or procedure manual. It should be noted as a function or department head. The auditor should search that this function or the person is clearly a member of auditee's own management. A consultant would not be a management representative. A clerk in the front office does not fit the definition. The auditor should review the organizational chart or look for the designation in the documentation. Does the management representative report on the condition of the quality system? When you are reviewing the management review records, ask "How does the management representative report on the performance of the system and is there a section in the continuous improvement program for input?" This question should be easily answered by the auditee if this function is in compliance.

The audit interview should begin with a review of the policy or procedure of the auditee with the "Executive" present. The audit plan should request a list of policies and procedures with the latest revision dates. Refer and read the section of management responsibility. If you did not perform the document review audit, then you need to familiarize yourself with the policy and objectives. Later in the audit you should view the objectives listed in the Business Plan and discussed in the Management Review.

The objective evidence of the Management Review is the record of the review. These records could be any type of form depending upon the organization. The essential items in the record will be a review of the internal audit, customer complaints, internal corrective actions, continuous improvement, strategic quality objectives, cost of poor quality, employee motivation measurements, delivery status to all customers, internal and external parts per million, and all the elements of the quality system. This is usually a brief overview for the top management person(s). A more detailed review will come during the analysis of the company level data.

The management review should contain any out of the ordinary problems with the auditee's customers. In the review of the customer performance data, you should look for any unusual occurrences of complaints, plant shut downs, containment's, or poor quality and delivery ppms. As an added inquiry, look at long term data for a year or six months to gain a better perspective of the condition of the system. A recent review of the last month is too short a time interval. Look into previous management review records. An added note would be to see what are the defined intervals for the management review. If the review is conducted once per month, then ask to see the previous six or twelve months of records. A review of these records should yield to the auditor a good view that the auditee is keeping to what is documented. In review of all of these records, you will also confirm that the retention times specified in element 4.16 are also in compliance. Be sure to check the policy or procedure of the 4.16 element for retention of these records.

Responsibility and authority of resources are usually audited during the document review audit. The auditee will provide either a matrix of interrelated responsibilities and authorities or these will be described in a separate section of the policy manual. In some cases, the procedure manual will list responsibilities in the beginning of the procedure. Look through these sources for the responsibility for disposition of nonconforming product and the customer representative. This is only a sampling, but it does accomplish the fact that these responsibilities have been documented and defined. Most importantly, the resources needed for quality should be defined for shifts and to stop production. Each shift shall be staffed with personnel responsibility for quality. This does not mean that these people report to the quality department, but that they have responsibility for quality. The auditor should ask if these same people have the authority to stop production for quality problems. This is to be defined and documented somewhere in the policy of procedure manuals. The names or the functions should be known to the auditor when the audits of the manufacturing or production areas are to be audited.

Resource requirements are not only related to personnel and training. There are times during an audit that an auditor will find that a person or a department does not have the proper tools, equipment, documents, or gages in order to perform their job or duties. This is usually found during the on site audit of the manufacturing where an operator does not have a gage or a work or test instruction is not available. These are shortcomings that management is to provide to its personnel.

Analysis and use of company level data can be a large section of the audit of Management and also an extension of the management review record. This section is factual management or what used to be called management by the facts. Certain key indicators are selected by the auditee for review on a periodic basis. The period is most frequently used is monthly. If the auditee is a FORD MOTOR COMPANY supplier, then the QOS system is to be used. This is a requirement of FORD and should be realized during the document review. The document review is done prior to the on site audit and must provide all information on customer specifics. Productivity as an indicator can take the form of first time quality. This is a measure of yield in the production process. It is normally designated in internal ppms (parts per million) or quantity of rejects at final or inprocess inspection. Cost of poor quality is a measure of the internal and external failure costs. These costs for rework and sorting charges in the plant due to nonconforming product rejections and the costs associated with returns to the plant for repair or rework. The external costs can also be for travel to a customer's plant to sort or rework. Quality indicators can be the internal ppms, quantity of internal corrective actions, number of noncompliance's on internal and external audits, and objectives for quality that are also in the Business Plan. Delivery to all customers is to be implemented and improved if delivery is not to 100%. Compare this indicator to the customer performance reports. Inventory control is another indicator that can be done using the inventory turnover ratio or total cost of inventory. This also satisfies the requirement of inventory management that is stated in sub element 4.15.3.2 of the standard. The business objectives from the business plan are another source. These objectives for achieving quality are from the sub element 4.1.1.2 in the standard. The objectives could be the attaining of personnel resources, training programs, or purchasing of new equipment. One of these objectives is to be the measurement of employee satisfaction and empowerment, sub element 4.1.6. The actual process of measurement might take place from the Human Resource function, but the results should be known by management in the management review. All of these objectives to achieve quality are to be in the business plan. Quality system performance in sub element 4.2.8, require recorded minimum evidence as objectives in the quality policy, business plan, and customer satisfaction. The first two have been mentioned above. Customer satisfaction, sub element 4.1.1.3, states that the indicators to monitor trends of satisfaction and dissatisfactions are to be done. The documented trends could be ppms, quantity of customer complaints, delivery, warranty returns, or customer plant shut downs. This is part of a documented process in Customer Satisfaction of this sub element. The auditor should ask to see where this process is documented and the frequency of determination established and performed.

All of these facts, indicators, or data are to be documented in trends that can be monitored for review of the complete system. The indicators are to be compared to the business objectives. Goals should be established as a comparison to the business plan or appropriate benchmarks. The establishment of these target goals serves as guide to the auditee as to the progress of the system. The auditor should review these indicators along with the goals to see if they are in a positive direction. If any of the trends is unfavorable or is not at the goal, then a corrective action should be in place. Sub element 4.1.5 of the standard requires out for a development of priorities for prompt solutions. Sub element 4.14.1.2 (problem solving) states that when an internal or external nonconformity to specification or requirement occurs, then the problem solving method is to be used. Certainly, if any of these indicators, which are key to the business, are not in the correct manner, then there should be a corrective action documented and a priority established. The auditor should ask to see these corrective actions when it is detected that the indicators are not to the internal requirement of the auditee. These indicators also include those of continuous improvement projects.

Continuous Improvement is noted in two (2) sub elements of the standard. The first is in 4.1.1.4 and the second in 4.2.7. The auditee must identify opportunities for improvement is a requirement. Guidelines for these opportunities can be found in note 1 of the standard and ISO-9004. These opportunities are to be in the quality policy that is also in the business plan. This is a connection to sub element 4.1.1.2. Also in sub element 4.2.7, Process Improvement is noted as continuous improvement in product characteristics with the highest priority on spe-cial characteristics. A prioritized plan is to be developed. The auditor should ask to see the prioritized plan of all of the continuous improvement activities. At the top of the list will be the special characteristics of the product and/or process. What does this mean? Sub element 4.2.4.7 states that special characteristics are to be in on all process control documents. These characteristics are usually designated by customers on the drawing (design record) or special communication to the supplier by the customer. The characteristics could be designated by the supplier in the form of product or process items. The main focus is one that the plan has these characteristics at the top of the plan and that the plan is prioritized for action items.

Continuous improvement is an ongoing effort. The auditor should see previous closed projects that were successful and sometimes there are projects that were not so successful. The main point is that is there a method to measure the progress of each project to achieve a measure of improvement to help the firm in business. Again this links us to the business plan. The continuous improvement projects should be included in the business plan. Per the sub element 4.1.1.2, the policy of the firm should be in the business plan. The methods used are not so much important as the end goals to achieve are measurable. In the case the significant characteristics, the capability indices should be above 1.33 CpK. If the index is below 1.33, then a corrective action plan should be in place. See the sub element 4.9.3 for a better explanation. This is not a continuous improvement project. Also, the index of using PpK is for unstable processes. CpK can only be used for stable processes. The auditor should see actions on how to improve these characteristics by way of variation reduction or decrease the sample size and frequency of the checks. If the capability of a process is at a CpK of 3.0 or higher and the control charts show a stable process with all special causes eliminated or identified, then the supplier should look into reducing the frequency of the checking. This reducing of the frequency can free up personnel to perform other tasks that could be more important to the firm.

Practical tips for the auditor are given here are derived from experience from other colleagues in the auditing business. These tips are of a practical nature and have a foundation of real experiences with auditees during audits. Some of these tips are notorious stall tactics to delay the auditor from completing the audit properly and on time.

"Let me give you an overview of the company and how far we have come to achieve world class quality in our organization" This statement will most likely come from the CEO or President of the firm. The intention is good, but the result is a waste of time to the auditor. There is a plan to execute and only a limited amount of time to complete it. A good response to this tactic is to ask if this will only take 10 minutes or less. A friendly reminder to the person that there is a time constraint usually cuts this item short to the 10 minutes or cancels the "Dog and Pony Show".

"What do you mean by Management Review or records?" "No one has ever asked for that information before?" If this is the first or the second audit for the auditee, then these questions are normal do to the unfamiliarity to the standard's requirements. However, if this is the fifth or ninth surveillance audit, this is a stall tactic to prolong the time. A reply could be that this is your fifth or the ninth audit and that you should know what is required. If the required information or records are not received in the allotted time, then write a noncompliance. There will probably be a protest from the auditee that the auditor wrote the noncompliance too quickly and did not listen. A simple explanation that when the required information if produced, then the noncompliance will become void and not included in the audit. The key phrase "when the required information is produced", is the qualifier to void the noncompliance. If the information is not produced, then the noncompliance stands as being valid. Writing the noncompliance at the end of the allotted time send a signal to those that are being audited that they have to be prepared for your audit. Conducting your audit in a crisp, concise, and thorough manner is an indicator of professionalism.

An additional item that may be asked in the management review, is the Impact on Society sub element, 4.1.7 This could be covered in the Human Resources department or Safety. Management should be aware of the safety consequences and it should be a part of the company policy. Many times, the use of company data reflects loss due to injuries as lost time and there is a goal to attain to minimize. In the audit of the manufacturing areas, the auditor should observe safety posters, results of days of safe operation in the plant or department, or posted graphical representations of the success of the safety program.

During the audit of management, the auditor should collect certain records of information to show compliance. There may be some disagreement among auditors or registrars about the collection of the records. Please remember that this book is only one method. It is not the "definitive" reference for all auditing to all standards. The information to be collected is as follows:

• Management Review record(s)

• Continuous Improvement Projects and results of improvement

- Customer Performance reports or data

- A list of all customer complaints for the last 6 or 12 months

- Copies of measurable data from the company

Some of this data may be proprietary in nature. Avoid collecting this data. Also, do not collect data that relates to financial information or advanced marketing data.

The order that is presented for the audit of this function is not important or does it has to be done at one time. The objective is to complete this sedation to gain a perspective of the management function. There could many people to interview in order to obtain the objective evidence required. The auditor is to be perserverant in the pursuit.

V.
Sales Function

The sales function in some organizations may be actually the sales personnel belonging to the firm. In other firms, the sales function could be the contracted sales representatives. These personnel are not connected to the audited firm. They are a subcontracted supplier. They probably are not aware of the requirements of ISO/TS-16949. The audit of this function would not be warranted. The function that performs contract review is the particular function that is needed. This could be Engineering who does the feasibility reviews and cost estimates. This is all dependent upon the size of the firm you are auditing.

The elements of the standard that apply to the Sales function are 4.2, 4.3, 4.4, 4.5, 4.7, 4.14, and 4.16. Each of the interrelationships of these elements and sub elements will be explained in the ensuing development of this chapter. The main objective to be learned is the many facets of the standard that apply to all functions of the firm. The Quality function is not the entire theme for this standard or any related standard.

During the opening meeting or during the audit of Sales, ask to see a list of the new projects that are being quoted. Usually the Sales function knows quote log. The review of the contract or request for quote is performed before acceptance of the purchase order. In some cases the auditee will get an order without a request for quote. The review process is the same. All requirements desired by the customer are to be met. Ask to see the request for quote or the purchase order. Review the requirements that are requested such as delivery dates, special packaging, special tests, traceability, regulatory requirements, shipping carriers, and the sample submission date. Some, all, or none of these items will be detailed. If there are none, then ask how were the customer requirements defined and documented. The company has to produce something for the customer and the technical function, engineering and production, need to know what to produce. A feasibility review is to be documented and recorded. Ask to see the record of this review. These records can vary in content so there has to be some latitude exercised by the auditor. Does the review meet the intent of defining the customer's requirements and have all sections of the requirements been addressed by a multi-functional team. A team can be two (2) or more people depending upon the size of the company being audited. The requirements from this review of feasibility and requirements of the customer are inputs to the product and process design. These functions will be covered in more detail in later chapters.

A supplement to the this quotation process is an identified process for cost elements. This is the estimate of labor, overhead, and material to produce the product. This is usually performed by an engineering estimator or someone in the accounting department. It could be done by the owner if the firm is small. The objective is to view the process not the data. Cost data are sensitive information to the auditee. Care and caution is to be exercised when asking for this data or the process. Actual data for a particular project is not essential to audit, but there is to be a process to produce this data. Substitute data can be viewed or a blank sheet of an estimation process. Sometimes the auditee will show the auditor the worst product that has been quoted.

Parallel to the product and process design phases, the Sales function can add input to these processes. This is accomplished retrieving warranty data on surrogate parts, PPM reports, customer complaints, and the use of Quality Function Deployment. Ask to see how the Sales personnel add input to these processes. A truly multidisciplinary approach would include the links to the customer. The Sales/Marketing function is the external link to the environment of the business world. Their input is vital for improving continually and for innovation. The product realization process also refers to the organizational interfaces. The inputs are to be defined and documented. This is stated in sub element 4.4.3 of the standard. Ask how is this accomplished and how does the Sales/Marketing function contribute.

Open issues on the progress of the planning process should be known by this function. It is especially important if the customer is involved. How are changes made before and after the product is in production? There are four(4) sections of the standard state that this is to be done. The sales function should know about an amendment to the contract and how it is distributed to other functions. In addition to this, documentation control requires a procedure for timely review of customer engineering standards and changes. Subelement 4.4.9 require all changes to be approved and 4.13.4 requires customer approval even for subcontractors. Which of the four does the sales function know and participate?

Continuous improvement is to be all pervasive throughout the firm. The sales function should have certain projects for continuous improvement. Some of these could be the response time to quotations, reduction of prices, cost control, warranty reductions, and decreased of customer complaints. Does the sales function know about any customer complaints and what is their role in helping to resolve them?

When the contracts are reviewed, are the considerations for customer supplied product known? This product could be in the form of tooling, dunnage, material, components, gages, test equipment, or production equipment. The contract may state that there is a maintenance agreement for the equipment. The contract or purchase order should be read and investigated if these items have been addressed.

The auditor should always audit the element 4.16 to see what is the retention period for the contract review records. This element only states that the retention period is to be defined. Investigate as to how long the records are retained. Select a random group of part numbers that are currently being shipped, and ask to see the contract review records.

As the audit of this function is being performed, keep in mind that there must be some flexibility about the function. Not all of the above items will be done by the Sales/Marketing function. If this is true, then ask where or who does know. If the sales people, do not know, then ask your guide.

VI.

Engineering—Product Design

This chapter takes up the engineering function from the design responsible auditee. The definition of a design responsible supplier is stated in the glossary A-18. This is a supplier that has the authority to establish of change an existing product specification for product delivered to a customer. Customer approval is always required for any changes. The related customer specifics will dictate what is the approved form or vehicle to obtain this approval. At present, General Motors requires a PAA, FORD uses an SREA, and Daimler Chrysler has an SRPC. All of these abbreviations are covered in the PPAP manual. Customers other than those listed above also have their respective procedures and forms for approval.

During the opening meeting, ask the management representative or the entire group what new projects or products are currently being considered in the planning process. As mentioned in the chapter on auditing Sales, these projects have been through the contract review process and are ready for project management. Design and Development Planning are the main focus of this chapter. Product Realization will be covered in a subsequent chapter. Product Realization encompasses both design and non-design responsible suppliers.

Select two(2) to three(3) projects or products to audit. If time allows, then go on to another. Find out who is the project leader or manager. This person is usually in the engineering department or is an engineer, but this may not always be the case. It is required to have plans for each activity. The person that the auditor is interviewing should have some form of a timing plan. The plan essentially describes a "who, what, and when". Review the procedures for the engineering function. This is to verify that these procedures are in compliance to the standard and to the actual implementation. Ensure that the procedure being reviewed is documented controlled to the master list or equivalent. The plan contains essential elements that are required. The elements are the design inputs, organizational interfaces, design outputs, design reviews with records, design verification, and validation. All of these essential elements may come in various forms on the plan.

The auditor should have the experience and knowledge to look for them. If they are not readily apparent, then the auditor should overtly ask for them.

The design inputs come from the contract review process in the form of drawings, sketches, letters, specifications, models, or whatever is necessary to communicate the customer's requirements. Along with these inputs is the feasibility study. Ask to see that this has been performed. If the recorded study shows that there are open issues, then ask how these issues have been resolved. The design project may be influenced by these issues. It is the responsibility of the auditee to resolve the issues. There should be objective evidence that this has been done. Examine the inputs to obtain a knowledge of what is required. The inputs need to be documented in some form. Reliability objectives are required as an input. See how these objectives are documented and how they will be achieved in the plan. There might be some required customer items to the input. Ask to see the purchase order so that the auditor can establish which items are to be in the inputs. These items could be in the form of special training or required skills for the engineering function. The audit for the required skills is usually performed in the Human Resources function. Ask where are the training records for the engineering function's required skills.

Examine the plan in detail to determine if the required objectives or milestones have been completed as to the timeline. The design plan is to be updated as the project or design evolves. If this project or the product is a similar item that the auditee has done before, then ask what is the process to utilize information to these similar projects. This is called use of information in the standard. In the plan ask to see various items that have been done. The organizational interfaces, other functions or outside subcontractors, are to be defined and documented. If this has been done, then ask to see the objective evidence of this completed event. Examples of these interfaces are meetings with subcontractors for tooling, materials, prototypes, drawings(CAD), design help, manufacturing, painting, plating, heat treating, and testing. As the auditor discovers who are the subcontractors, make notes to check with purchasing to see if these are approved subcontractors by their procedure or process. This approval process is required in subelement 4.6.2.1 of the standard. This is an appropriate time to ask if there is access to research and development facility. This interface may be present in the design plan. If prototypes are required, then there should be a prototype control plan. Usually the requirement for prototypes is covered in the purchase order or a special request from the customer. In these instances a prototype control plan is warranted. In the use of tools or tooling sources, ask how the tools will be marked with the customer ownership if the customer is paying for the tools. In addition, if the tools are sourced to a subcontractor how is the confidentiality maintained for the project. This is noted in subelement 4.2.4.1. In the materials area ask about the regulatory regulations for any and all materials as described in subelement 4.6.1.3. Some of these questions may be part of another function(s) and cannot be answered by the engineer or the engineering manager. If this is the case, then make notes to visit the correct functions or inform the other auditor(s) to inquire as to the answers for these questions.

The design outputs can take on many forms. All of these forms must be documented and expressed in terms that can be verified to the input requirements. All of the out put documents are to be reviewed before release. This means that drawings are signed off for approval. Specifications are document controlled and approved. Test data has been reviewed and accepted. There are acceptance standards created and approved. The approvals should come from a qualified source. Ask who is responsible for the approvals, then check if all of the approvals are from the aforementioned sources. Product parameters are to be monitored in production as specified in element 4.9.d. Have these parameters been created by engineering and what are they? Packaging standards, if not specified by the customer, should be created and approved. The product is to be protected as per 4.15.6.1 during delivery to the customer. What provisions have been made to ensure that the packaging is acceptable to the customer? One of the most important outputs of engineering is the Design Failure Modes and Effects document. There is a point in the plan, usually before the design process begins, when the DFMEA is created. This requires a core team that could be sales, subcontractors, manufacturing, tooling engineering, industrial engineering, and management. One of the factors is that of design for manufacturing or assembly. Ask if this consideration has been taken into account. Has the design been optimized to reduce waste or add value to the production process? There should be some objective evidence of these factors from the design team.

Ask to see the DFMEA if it has been completed according to the timing plan. DFMEAs are required for all new and carryover parts. Examine the document for the following items:

1. Who are the members of the team and are they multidisciplined?

2. When was the fmea created? It should be early in the design process.

3. What is the design level? This is to be in the item/function sedation.

4. Are the failure modes clear in physical and technical terms?

5. Are the effects of the failures specific as perceived by the customer?

6. What is the severity number and is it justified?

7. Are all significant and/or critical characteristics on the fmea? See the drawing.

8. Are the causes clear and unambiguous?

9. Is there an occurrence number?

10. Do the current design controls contain the preferred defect prevention mode?

11. Are the risk priority numbers, RPNs, rank ordered for reduction of the highest number? Check for recommendations.

12. Is responsibility assigned for the reduction of the highest RPNs and a timing date for completion?

13. If the actions have been completed for the reduction of the high RPNs, is there a new RPN calculated?

Returning to the timing plan, the auditor should review the plan to see if there are formal design reviews scheduled. As the evolution of the design process proceeds, at certain key intervals, a review is necessary. These are to be planned and are to be in the timing plan for the project. The auditor is to review a record of these reviews. Records are to be documented and will be part of the retained records in element 4.16. Check that these are a part of the 4.16 element and how long they are retained. When reviewing the record, look for who are the attendees at the review. Appropriate functions are to be represented. If the review is conducted after receiving outside sourced tooling or components, then some of the participants could be the subcontractors of the tooling or components. The reviews are to be formal and in the plan.

Additionally in the plan there is a record(s) of the verification of the design. The record verifies that all of the outputs meet the inputs. This record can be in various forms, but the most common is the aforementioned design review record. Accompanying this record is usually a list of open issues with responsibilities and due dates. This open issue list can be incorporated into the revised design plan. The verification stage also might include test reports that are required by the drawing or tests proposed by the design engineer(s). There is an acceptance criteria for these tests. Commonly this record of tests and result is the Design Verification Plan and Record, D.V.P.& R. Check that all tests required by the design record (drawings, specifications, catia sheets, etc.)Are on the plan and if completed, what are the results. If the results do not meet the acceptance criteria, then there is a corrective action. The corrective action is to be in accordance to the 4.14.1.2, the disciplined problem solving method adopted by the auditee. This is called a design failure in the standard. However, it is more appropriate to call these results test failures. The auditor may not be qualified to pass judgment on the entire design. Some design engineers become upset when someone calls their design a failure. The validation stage has not been reached and the corrective action to the "test failures" will correct the discrepancy.

This brings us to the Validation stage. Validation records show that the product(s) conform to what the customer desires. Usually this validation is the PAP process required by the customer for sample submission and approval. This validation should coincide with the customer's timing plan. The auditee's design plan, at most times, includes the sample submission date to the customer. The sample submission process, PAP subelement 4.2.4.11, will be discussed in the chapter on Quality.

The audit of the Engineering function must include a review of the documentation control of drawings, specifications, and design changes. The note in subelement 4.5.2.1 describes appropriate documents that are controlled. Obtain the master list of these controlled documents. Select drawing numbers that are controlled and ask to see the current document. Check the drawing to the revision date on the master list to see if they match. While reviewing the drawing, look for required tests and ask to see the record of completion. Specifications noted on the drawing, should be controlled and on site for the auditee's personnel. While reviewing the related specifications, ask to see the test reports or data that is required by the specification. Carefully view the entire drawing(s) or related design records(catia sheets, cad drwgs., and documents) to discover any significant and/or critical characteristics. If these characteristics are present, then ask to see the control plans, fmeas, procedures, work instructions, and forms. All of these documents are to have the designated characteristics noted on them. See subelement 4.2.4.7 for the exact requirement. Continue with a random sample of many drawings or specifications asking the same questions for objective evidence as noted in the above. Ask to see the procedure for review of engineering standards or specifications or changes. This procedure is required by subelement 4.5.2.2. A record of the date of the changes is to be maintained in retained records. Again, see the element 4.16 to see if this is an identified retained record and for how long. The review is to be timely and the recorded date of implementation is to be noted. See how long is the interval before the change or specification has been implemented. The note in subelement 4.5.2.2 describes this timing in days. A maximum required time would be nine(9) days.

Design changes are to be recorded for product and process. The design changes are to be documented and approved by authorized personnel. When reviewing these design changes, ask who are the authorized personnel to approve the changes. See if the correct personnel have approved the change. If there is a change that affects the design, then there should be a written authorization from the customer. This is related by the subelement 4.13.4, engineering approved authorization. Any change that deviates from what is currently approved requires a written authorization. The glossary definition, A22, defines engineering approved authorization as written authorization required whenever the product or process varies from those currently customer approved. Any change in a sub-contractor or the subcontractor's process is included. The customer approved authorization is the Product Approval Process, subelement 4.2.4.11. Review the changes for proper approvals through the PAP or other vehicle used by the customer. If these written authorizations are not in evident, then ask to see a customer waiver. In all cases the auditee should evaluate and validate all changes to the product and the process.

In conclusion, the auditor should view auditing the design engineering function with a measure of flexibility. Many engineering functions operate in different modes and methods. The complexity of the project or product should be taken into account when auditing. A simple project such as a single die stamping would have a timing plan of one page in length with only one design review. A full ABS brake system would have multiple timing charts or critical path method charts to plan. The design reviews would multiple at various stages of the design evolution. The entire plan could take three years to complete. Examine the product or project to be produced.

VII.
Engineering—Process Design

Process design or process engineering takes on many different names for manufacturing. Some of the many names are production, industrial, process, or manufacturing engineering. All of these names and disciplines follow the engineering of the process of manufacturing to produce a product. A product is a tangible or intangible object. A definition of product, A.45 in the glossary, is the result of activities or process. The standard for QS-9000 for this topic is the AIAG A.P.Q.P. Manual. The 16949 standard is the element 4.2.4, Product Realization. This is the planning and management of activities up to and including part approval. Unlike product design, in the previous chapter, this is the total project management of an entire project. The product design plan is a subset of this plan. For those auditees who are not design responsible, this is the planning for the product. The components of this process are the feasibility study, contract review, management of process design, control plans, failure modes and effects analysis, facility layout, tooling management, maintenance program, reports, and feedback appraisal to management.

The first step in auditing this function is to obtain a list of current projects at the opening meeting. This is a similar technique that was mentioned in the chapter on product design. The Lead auditor should assign a person with experience in project management. Those auditors who are familiar with the A.P.Q.P process will understand this process. The most common approach to Product Realization is the use of a project management program. A project leader is assigned and a team is formed. The auditor should question the composition of the team. It should be multifunctional or multidisciplined. If there is a plan of events in the project management (who, what, and when), examine the plan for review and feedback to management. This provides a status report to keep management appraised of the progress. The plan is to have appropriate points where events are measured to assess the progress of the project. These are usually dates to be achieved along the critical path of the project. The auditor should look to see if these dates or milestones have been achieved. If these dates are behind the intended goal, then an action plan is to be in place. Ask to see this action plan, if it is required by the late dates.

The management of process design (4.2.4.9) of a specific project is to have a feasibility review recorded. This occurs at the contract review stage and should be documented in some sort of form declaring that the organization can meet the requirements of the customer. Examine this feasibility to understand the customer requirements. Look to see who is the customer and ask if the auditee understands all of the customer's requirements or has the customer's manual. There are certain customers that desire an update to the project management plan on a periodic basis. See if this update is included in the plan. The auditor should read the customer's purchase order for specific requirements such as prototypes, computer aided design, significant characteristics for SPC, packaging, or sample submission date. Again, look for these requirements on the plan or if they have been considered. While this is also covered in the contract review audit, the auditor that is auditing the process engineering function should also audit to this level. If there are two auditors, then this serves as an overlapping check.

The process design inputs are to be documented and may consist of drawings and specifications from the customer, regulations and environmental concerns, or specific customer requirements. How are these inputs documented? If the drawings and specifications are on a CAD program, then ask to see the CAD data. Also make note of who is the CAD operator. This operator's records should be on file to demonstrate training or qualified status for the CAD operation. Outputs from the design function are usually in the form of the drawings and specifications. Ask for the design FMEA, if the auditee is design responsible. The auditor should examine it for correctness to the particular customer's manual. If the project is for one of the Big Three, then this requirement is the AIAG FMEA manual. If there is another customer, then the auditor should ask what is the particular requirement for FMEAs from that customer. Obtaining a customer DFMEA is a rare occurrence. They are usually confidential or do not exist. Other inputs to the process development could be auditee requirements as per there manual. Read the particular procedures to discover what may be an internal requirement. These internal requirements may be on the plan or documented in some manner. Ask to see the objective evidence that complies with the auditee's required procedure.

Process design outputs are in varied forms to show that the inputs have been achieved and are in a tangible form. Subelement .4.2.4.9.4 requires that a record be retained to demonstrate evidence of compliance. This is noted in the standard as the process verification record. This record can be the completion dates in the timing plan. Ask to see the objective evidence that these items have been completed and exist. One of the important items is the protection of confidentiality of the customer's project or product. If the auditee has subcontracted outside services, then there should be a process to protect the customer or the auditee's product. This could be a confidentiality agreement between the subcontractor and the auditee. If this is the process, then ask to see these agreements from the list of available subcontractors that are employed by the auditee. The product realization outputs will include the use of PFMEAs for the process. If there are no other requirements for other customers in regards to the PFMEAs, then refer to the AIAG's manual for FMEAs. There are many requirements for the fulfillment of a correct PFMEA. The PFMEA is usually conducted before the feasibility stage and prior to tooling arrangements. A flow chart assessment is performed to outline the various sources of variation and risk. The failure mode is the discrepancy to meet the process requirements and is described in objectively. The effects of the failure take into account all of the customers. The ultimate customer as well as the immediate customer downstream from the process. These are related in terms of the process performance. The potential causes are described as what could occur and can be corrected. The causes are specific to the problem. Do not use vague or ambiguous terms. Seek out the possible or real causes and document them thoroughly. The current process controls should coincide with those of the control plan or associated documents. These controls should be of a preventive nature. The use of the rankings of the RPN numbers is to be done with caution. Severity is the seriousness of the effect. Too many times the auditee will select a high severity(7,8,9, or 10) where it is not justified. The use of a severity of 9 or 10 means that there is potential of a violation of a government regulation and that failure is without or with warning. In short, people may die or become seriously injured. Be cautious with the selection of this number. The occurrence is the projected frequency of the failure. This, like all of the numbers, is a combination of subjective and objective probabilities. The detection is the probability that the current process controls will detect the failure. Too many times the auditee will assign a low number to a control that is not justified. The selection of a "1" means that there is complete certainty that the defect will be detected. A "1" means that there is a "poke-yoke" or "fail-safe" device in the process to catch all defects. It behooves the auditee to examine all of these numbers for their correctness in application. The auditor should examine the right side of the PFMEA for reduction of RPN numbers and recommended actions. The FMEA is a living document that is updated every time there is a failure not noted or a change to the process. Many times the auditee will document recommended actions, but not follow up with the completion and recalculation of the RPNs. The FMEA for the process is rank ordered for reduction of the RPNs. This is similar to DFMEA mentioned in the previous chapter. The reduction of these RPNs is a very good source for continuous improvement in the design and process.

Other outputs that are likely are the creation of work instructions for new processes, acceptance criteria for processes, required recorded data to prove compliance to the required criteria. The culmination of the product realization process is the Product Approval Process. The Big "3" will use the AIAG-PPAP manual. Other customers will have their own version of product approval before the first production shipment. It is required that the auditee know what is the particular requirements for all customers and communicate these requirements to the auditor. This was covered in an earlier chapter. We will cover the AIAG-PPAP manual since it is used by the Big "3" as the source of initial product approval. There are some important points to cover about the PAP requirement that are not always known by the auditee(supplier). The standard states that this approval process applies to subcontractors that the auditee uses in the production of the samples. This means that all of the requirements in the manual, recognized by the customer, that the auditee has evidence also applies to the subcontractors. All of the evidence is to be on hand from the subcontractors. There should be control plans, FMEAs, flow charts, lab tests, dimensional layouts, and a warrant. All changes are to be validated by the auditee. This also includes changes by the subcontractor. The customer is to be notified of all of the changes. Changes that deviate from the current approved product and/or process require written customer approval. Subelement 4.9.3, states that there will be records of process changes and the effective dates. The auditor should ask for this record(s) of all of the process changes. If these changes are different from the current approved process, the latest PPAP, then there should be another PPAP or a customer notification waiver. The waiver is to be in writing with name and date. It is important to note that all changes are to be communicated to the customer. The auditee should not assume that the customer does not care or the change will not effect other processes unforeseen by the auditee. The AIAG-PPAP manual does list when the customer is to be notified. This applies to the Big "3", but other customers may be more or less particular about these changes. It is best to err on the conservative side of the decision process. The following list are common areas that incur nonconformances in the audit of a sample submission package:

• The warrant will not have the proper weight to 4 places in kilograms.

- The warrant will not have the correct revision level to the drawing.

- There is no part approval report when it is required by the drawing.

- Material and Performance reports do not come from a certified laboratory and there are blanket statements of conformity.

- The significant production run is less than 300 pieces and all molds/dies/lines are not represented.

- Dimensional results are missing from requirements on the drawing and some dimensions are blanket statements of conformity.

- Dimensional results are out of the drawing tolerance, but there is no indication described in the warrant declaration. (This is a Major noncompliance)

- Process flow diagrams do not follow the control plan or vice versa.

- There is no master sample or it is not identified.

- All required tests as stated by the design record(drawing) have not been performed.

- Significant characteristics, noted on the drawing, do not have control charts to demonstrate stability and/or capability results are less than required.

- Checking aids have not been checked for conformance and do not have the latest revision level corresponding to the drawing.

- Measurement System Analysis studies are not present and/or they exceed the requirements of the customer or supplier.

The above list is only a sampling of what has occurred during audits of PPAP submissions. The auditor should examine all of the nineteen subelements of the manual for conformance. The design record will be the governing factor to determining what is required as well as the respective manual of the customer.

This is not an exhaustive explanation of how to audit this item.

Plant, facility, and equipment planning is performed during the Product Realization process and is usually noted on the timing plan. If there is a new process or piece of equipment, it should be put on the floor diagram as to where it will be located. Along with this there should be objective evidence that existing operations have been evaluated for effectiveness. Some of this evidence will be in the form of a continuous improvement program such as "lean manufacturing" events. These events take into account the factors of ergonomics, floor space, throughput time, and value added content. The auditor should look for these items in the audit of product realization or continuous improvement. The sections of the standard are not stand alone items to be audited and checked on a "grocery" list mentality. All of these items are inter linked in the operations and planning. The auditor should be cognizant of all of the input stimuli during the audit. Just because the auditor is in the engineering area, does not mean there will be audit trails in other areas. Make copious notes if necessary to follow up on these trails.

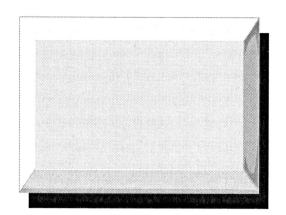

VIII.
Purchasing/Materials

The audit of the purchasing function is begun by asking for a list of approved subcontractors during the opening meeting. The standard does not state that there has to be such a list, but usually the auditee has such a list that is used by the purchasing manager or buyers. The auditor should review this list to see if appropriate subcontractors should be on the list. Many times this list will be just a listing of anybody or organization that a check is written on for payment. If this is true, then inform the auditee that subcontractors such as a traffic court payment or catered lunch bill will be audited for evaluation. This is an indication to the auditee of where the auditor is going during the audit. If the list cannot or will not be corrected, then cover these evaluations during the interview in the purchasing office. This will be explained later in this chapter.

Obtain the procedure for Purchasing and read it through making notes of various items of importance. Some of these items could be the evaluation reports issued on subcontractors, when corrective action is required for quality or delivery infractions, or the method of obtaining approval from the purchasing function. Is the procedure the latest and controlled? Check the master list or equivalent for this document control. In this way the auditor will check the document control element as well as the Purchasing function. In all such audits, the routine is the same. Always check that the policy, procedure, or work instruction are controlled to the latest level. In this way the auditor combines the document control element with the function being audited. The goal is to observe evidence that the procedure or work instruction has been implemented. The auditor has to see objective evidence that the implementation has been performed.

The auditor should look for some sort of a performance report on the approved subcontractors. The procedure will describe how the evaluations are performed and recorded. Using the approved subcontractor list or the equivalent, ask to see the individual performance reports of selected subcontractors. The auditor should look for consistency in the application of the procedure. Additionally, there should be a report for on time delivery of the subcontractors. If there are late deliveries, then ask when is corrective action required? These criteria for corrective action should be documented in the policy or procedure or work instruction. Investigate if this criterion is being implemented by asking for the corrective actions when the data warrants. Many times the reports from the Quality function or receiving inspection will ask for corrective action for defective product. If this is documented in the procedure, then ask to see those corrective actions. When reviewing the corrective actions, observe if they are within the time frame required by the auditee. Another question to the auditee is how are these requirements of delivery to 100% and quality conveyed to the subcontractors? They, the requirements, could be in the procedure, but how does the subcontractor know of them? Usually this is a "boiler plate" statement on the purchase order or there is a separate letter to all subcontractors or there is a subcontractor quality manual. The auditor needs to see objective evidence of how these requirements are communicated. This also is the case for releases on "blanket" purchase orders. In the data analysis phase, there should be a notation or reconciling for premium freight inbound. This can be done in many ways. It is up to the auditor to see that premium freight is being tracked either by money or occurrence. Outside procured tests and calibrations are to come from accredited laboratories. The glossary defines these laboratories as being approved by a nationally recognized accreditation body such as A2LA, SCC, or COFRAC. Ask to see if these outside sources are evaluated and what is the criteria. The auditor should verify that these sources have the appropriate certificates. The quality function usually files the certificates in the lab. Sometimes the purchasing function keeps them in a file for each subcontractor. The definition of product is the result of activities or processes. It can be tangible or intangible including services and knowledge.

The selection of subcontractors is to be described in the documentation. How are new subcontractors put on the approved list or how are approved to be used? If there have been new subcontractors added to the approved status, what are the criteria and who are the latest approvals? Check the files for all of the new arrivals to see if they meet the documented criteria. Customer selected subcontractors are usually denoted on the design record(drawing) or are listed in the specific materials specification that is also on the design record. Make a note of the new subcontractors and check their record in the receiving inspection. There should be records of acceptable performance. There can be subcontractors that are not required to have their product inspected due to an acceptable record of performance. This can be accomplished by having a specified amount of shipments that have passed an inspection criteria defined by the auditee(supplier) or through repeated outside lab tests have performed well. In any event there has to be objective evidence that these acceptable records are retained. This is stated in element 4.16 of the standard and also referenced in subelements 4.6.2.1.b and 4.10.2.2. There are many times that an auditee will claim that "We do not do receiving inspection. All of our subcontractors are ISO or QS-9000 registered". This only covers half of one of the four required incoming product quality of subelement 4.10.2.4. This will be discussed more in the chapter for Receiving and Shipping.

Subcontractor development is required to ensure compliance to ISO/TS-16949. The auditor should use the approved list and ask what is the development program to any or all of the firms on the list. Some auditees(suppliers) require that all of their subcontractors be ISO registered. This might be compliant to a QS-9000 audit, but the standard states to this standard, which is ISO/TS-16949. The usual reply is that subcontractors are required to fill out a survey describing the quality system. The auditor should review the survey to see if the questions are part of the standard listed above. Many times the survey questions are too general or only ask requirements for an ISO standard. The survey may be in line with a customer system. If this is the case, then the auditor should ask to see what is the documentation for this system. Compare the questions to the aforementioned system. There is a guidance note number 2 in the standard that refers to prioritization. This means that the auditee(supplier) can perform the development based on a priority of need or of performance. If 95 % of all of the suppliers have zero p.p.m.s and are 100 % on time for delivery, then the auditee might concentrate on the 5% that are not in compliance. This a logical and value added approach.

Regulatory compliance, along the lines of ISO-14000, can be demonstrated in various ways. There are "boiler plate" requirements on the purchase orders stating that all regulatory requirements are to be in effect and that the subcontractor is to comply. This could mean that MSDS sheets are required with the first shipment or when the purchased is changed. The customer's design record(drawing) might also specify or the noted specifications will specify requirements. The auditor should take note of these areas when auditing other functions at a different time. When this is revealed in another area or function, then ask to return to the function that holds the proof of evidence. This is another audit trail to follow.

The role of the Purchasing/Materials in the Product Realization process is part of the multi-disciplined team effort. The auditor needs to determine what is this role by investigative questions to the function heads. Are customer designated subcontractors available and how does the Purchasing function know if they are required? If there are new additions to the approved list, has a PAP or approval been acquired by the customer using the customer's procedure? In the case of the "Big 3", this would be a PPAP approval. During the audit of the Product Realization Process in Engineering or Quality, the auditor should determine if there are new subcontractors and full approvals. Subelement 4.6.1.2 states that other subcontractors may be used after they have been approved by the customer. This approval is the PAP process that is located at subelement 4.24.11. During the contract review or project management of a new product or project, the question arises about packaging and shipping of the completed product. The subelement 4.15.4 and 4.15.6.1 require compliance to the customer's packaging standards and labeling. There could be returnable packaging involved. The auditor should ascertain how the Purchasing function handles this customer supplied product and the care of it. Along these same lines, this also applies to consignment of raw materials or components. The essential question is to determine how Purchasing knows about these items, communicates requirements to the subcontractors and the auditee's personnel, and the care and maintenance. Other factors are trace ability requirements from the customer's contract for regulatory items or safety items. Materials used in the interior of the vehicle are subject to a United States Federal Motor Vehicle Safety Standard 302. This requires that burn tests be conducted and pass a particular standard of acceptance. Has this been considered by the auditee and conveyed to the subcontractor supplying the material. Materials that are perishable need special storage conditions and frequent review of the areas of storage. Has this been considered and action taken to preserve these materials? The interrogative questioning may not reveal all the answers from this particular function. The questions should lead the auditor to discover if these conditions have been addressed by any of the functions of the auditee. Again these are audit trails for investigation by the auditor.

Purchasing documents shall be approved prior to release. Who is authorized to approve these documents? Subelement 4.5.2.1 states that approved documents are approved by authorized personnel. Who are these personnel not only for documentation control but also for Purchasing? Specifically, who can sign an approval for a purchase order? Normally each company will designate someone to authorize purchases. Sometimes there is a hierarchy of approvals depending upon the amount being spent. If this is the case, the auditor should carefully review these purchase orders for the correct person(s). It should be stated who is the authority somewhere in the policy or procedures or work instruction. The purchase orders are to be specific and clear to the subcontractor and to the auditor. Specific means that there should be a reference to a drawing, specification, or other requirement. Vague or ambiguous references should be questioned by the auditor as to their origin. The auditor should ask if this purchase is for a specific part number or series of parts. If this true, then ask to see the particular drawing and look for a specific requirement. The drawing will usually make a specific call out for material, coating, or treatment. Ask for the particular specification and the related requirements. These should be on the purchase order. However, there are time when the customer or the design function does not specify any particular requirement. Words such as "paint black" or "file hard" or "weld securely" are but a few of these exceptions. In these cases, the auditee is justified in the vague call out. The auditor might want to ask the auditee if these vague references were discussed during the Product Realization phase or Contract Review process in order to clarify the requirements. There have been occurrences when the requirements are specific, but the auditee has never inquired during these investigative phases. The result is that the customer makes changes that the auditee cannot meet.

Verification of product or service at the subcontractor's premises either by the supplier(auditee) or the customer is covered in auditee's policy or procedures and the customer's contract. The auditor is to review the documents and the contracts to verify that this has been done or is going to be done. The reference to the subelements needs to be documented.

The audit of the Purchasing/Materials function may also be extended to the areas of shipping, receiving, and production control. This is the case when this function is performed under one group. The audit of these elements will be discussed in another chapter. If the auditor finds "the all encompassing function" does include the other elements, then extend the audit time. Notify the lead auditor and the management representative. Modify the audit plan and inform the guide to notify any of the other functions of the changes. In all, the auditor is to ensure full compliance to the standard and the auditee's documents.

IX.
Shipping, Receiving, Scheduling, and Inventory

The four areas of shipping, receiving, scheduling, and inventory are treated as a single group. These are the inputs and outputs of the production/manufacturing process. This chapter will cover the receiving inspection function. These four areas are under the management of a Materials function in some organizations. The auditor should inquire as to the structure of the organization during the opening meeting or before the audit. This saves time and informs the auditee as to the scope of the audit.

Receiving and Receiving Inspection: The receiving area is audited for how material is received, stored, and appropriately dispatched or issued to the manufacturing function. The area or function should have a procedure or work instruction on how this receiving task is to be performed. The controlled documentation might state that the receiving person reviews the invoice or bill of lading to the purchase order to ensure that what was received is what was ordered. This is a common practice in most companies. The instruction might go on to state that the received invoice is to be signed after the receiving person has confirmed that all items are received and the date of receipt. The date of receipt is used in some companies as a means of tracking the on time delivery of the subcontractor for compliance to the sub element 4.6.2.3. This was discussed in the chapter on Purchasing. Along with the confirmation of the goods, there is a check for damage of the containers. In the case of customer supplied product, this is essential in order for contact to the customer. The auditor should observe all of these tasks during the audit. Ask the receiving person how the tasks are accomplished. If there are work instructions or a procedure, then check for the correct revision by referring to the master list. The auditor should observe if the person is doing what is documented. Check the invoices have been signed if this is a requirement in the documentation. Read the work instructions carefully and observe that all of the essential items are performed and that there are records to

51

show implementation. If there is time, ask to see old records. In the case of customer supplied product, ask if there is customer returnable packaging and have there been occurrences of damage. If this is true, then ask where is the documented evidence that the customer was notified. Verify that this is being done. If there is customer consigned material, then verify that this material is stored in a proper manner and also ask if there has been any damage to this consigned material.

When material is stored before release to the production areas, the auditor should check where are the designated storage areas. The auditor should observe that the areas are protected so that the material is not subjected to damage or deterioration from the weather or other sources. This is very important for adhesives, paint, tape, cloth fabrics, paper products, and chemicals. Read the labels of the products to see if there are expiration dates. Check that they have not expired. Ask the personnel in these areas if the products have been assessed for the deterioration or expiration date. There should be objective evidence to prove that this has been completed. For further investigation, ask to see the specification or MSDS sheets. Read these specifications and look for an expiration date or special storage instructions. There are some items on the MSDS sheets that do describe how the item is to be stored. If the designated areas are specifically numbered, then ask what is the location number and what product is in that location. This is usually done by a computer system for inventory purposes. Write down the numbers of the located areas and the product identification. Ask to locate these items in the inventory system computer. Ensure that they are in the correct locations and have the proper quantity. This check is a precursor to the inventory audit. There should be an authorized method to issue the product to the manufacturing area(s). This is called dispatch from the stored areas. The majority of the time, this is handled by an MRP method. Ask that this method be demonstrated for the auditor. Observe the handling methods in use. The methods are to be in such a manner so that there is no damage. Observe the stored items for damage from forklifts or careless stacking that has broken boxes. The area of receiving should be organized and clean for the particular product being produced.

Receiving inspection is stated in the sublements 4.10.2 through 4.10.2.4 and a reference from 4.6.2.1.a. The main focus of this function is the assurance of the received product is to the requirements of the purchase order contract. There are usually procedures or work instructions for the implementation of this task. Review these documents and check that they are the latest to the master list or equivalent. This is a documentation control check. As a side note, the checking of the documentation during the entire audit serves to audit the element 4.5(Document and Data Control) without deliberately auditing this element alone. This is to be performed at all functions during the audit. Receiving inspection from an automotive viewpoint is the sub element 4.10.2.4, Incoming Product Quality. There are four methods to be used. Waiver by the customer is rare in occurrence. The four methods will be discussed with references to the other sub elements. This is done to show the interaction of all of these items. Obtain the procedure or work instruction for this function/task and read what method is being incorporated. The receipt and evaluation of statistical data is performed when the subcontractor to the supplier is required to send such data. This is done when the customer or supplier has designated the significant characteristics on the drawing or specification. The common nonconformance here is the failure to evaluate the data received. Statistical data is histograms, run charts, x-bar & r charts, or any data that would be commonly listed in a Statistics textbook. It is not certificates of analysis or compliance. The failure to evaluate this data is that the data shows an unstable process or an incapable performance. The common mistake is to file the data and accept the product. The auditor should investigate if the data is actually being checked. Also check that the designated characteristics are the actually the items required.

Receiving inspection and/or testing is prevalent in most companies. The inspection is described in the work instruction or procedure. Here the fault is that the receiving inspector does not check all of the items required, select the correct sample size, or indicate if the lot received is accepted and by what authority. The use of MIL-STD-105 sampling tables is acceptable as long as the acceptance number is zero in all cases. Work instructions state that the use of this standard in some cases fail to stipulate that the acceptance number is zero. The inspector checks a lot with a large sample size only to use an acceptance number that is not zero. Those of you reading this that are familiar with this standard will understand the problem. Those that are not, please get a copy of the standard and read it. The auditor should look at the records and carefully audit that all of the required items are in fact being done. Pay particular importance to the tolerances and if the product meets the acceptance criteria. If there is an unacceptable entry(nonconforming product), ask who has the authorization to accept nonconforming material into the manufacturing process. If the acceptance of this nonconforming causes a final product dimension to be out of the required tolerance, then this is a major nonconformance. In this case the auditor should check if there is a written waiver from the customer. In any event, the inspection should follow the work instruction or procedure and the requirement of the standard. The auditor is to be diligent to ensure that this is being performed.

Second or third party assessments of subcontractor sites means that the customer or a certified registrar has audited the site. The auditor should obtain the certificate or report that these sites have indeed been audited. The third party audits can be to ISO-9000 or QS-9000. Observe the certificates for correct identification. This is only the first part of the requirement. These audits from the third and second parties must also have records of acceptable subcontractor performance. There must be objective evidence that subcontractors have been satisfactory to the requirements specified by the supplier. Many times these records have been actual inspection data of past compliance. These subcontractors go from "dock to stock" because there is a history of good past performance. There are suppliers(auditees) that have approved subcontractors without this past acceptable performance records. Certificates of analysis or compliance are not records of acceptable performance.

The evaluation by accredited laboratories can be accomplished by a yearly evaluation of the material. This can be an expensive method. An accredited laboratory is one that is reviewed and approved by a nationally recognized accreditation body. These bodies can be A2LA, COFRAC, or SCC or certified to ISO/IEC 17025. If this is the chosen method, then the auditor should ask to see objective evidence of the certificates. The auditor should always seek objective evidence to verify conformance. Only certain selected bodies can certify laboratories for accreditation to ISO/IEC-17025. The auditee and the auditor should obtain a list of these bodies to ensure that the labs contracted or being audited are properly accredited. There are many certificates claiming that the laboratory performs all tests to the principles of ISO/IEC-17025, but the lab is not accredited. There is a difference. The auditor should review the certificate to ensure that the body accrediting the laboratory has stated to the standard above.

The audit of the shipping area(s) is performed along with the receiving area or can be done separately. In small to medium size plants the shipping and receiving areas are the same or are close. In large plants they could be on opposite sides of the building or in separate buildings or separate cities. In any of the cases, the auditor should walk through the area to look at the general condition of housekeeping and orderliness. If there is an unkempt look about the area, then the auditor should start looking in the areas for unmarked boxes, broken boxes or skids, or closed areas in the back of the shipping area. These are common problems if the area is not organized. The auditor should look at the labels on the boxes or skids to see if they are proper. To know if the labels are correct, ask the auditee for the packaging standards required from the customer in question. Quickly review these requirements to see if the auditee has complied. The bar code labels for the "Big 3" contain the revision level of the product that is being shipped. Make note of these levels and check them to the current drawing and purchase order. This audit trail ensures that the auditee has a system to communicate changes to all functions. This is a requirement in elements 4.3, 4.4, and 4.5. If there is a large customer base, then the auditor should choose the largest customers. Look at the packaging and review the aforementioned requirements to ensure that the packing is correct. Are the boxes and skids the proper size for the requirement? Are returnable containers required? The auditor should check the contract (purchase order) to see if returnables are required. As mentioned before, the returnable containers are usually customer supplied product. The auditee will sometimes not have enough returnables to fulfill the customer's requirements or the customer has not returned the containers. The auditee will start using expendable (cardboard) boxes. Ask to see if this a viable alternative and has been approved by the customer. The auditor should check that there are work instructions for the shipping personnel. This is if the packaging is being performed in the shipping area. There are many times the packing is performed at the last manufacturing operation. If this is the case then look for instructions on how to properly pack the product.

The area of inventory and/or production control is in many organizations the same function. The distribution of work and control of the inprocess/finished goods inventory is performed by one function in small to medium sized companies. In large organizations, these functions are separate and located in different locations. The distribution of work can come under the sub element 4.9.1.1.a through g., 4.15.6.3, 4.1.2.4, 4.15.6.4, and 4.15.6.5. Essentially what type of communication is sent to the supplier(auditee) and does the supplier have the capability of receiving this communication. In almost all automotive applications, this is addressed in the contract review/feasibility study stages. When a quotation is proposed the customer requires the supplier(auditee) to have the necessary hardware and software to receive the released requirements. This also includes the shipment notification system of advanced shipment notices, ASNs. If the auditee is not using ASNs, then there should be an agreement for this requirement specified by the customer. Check to see that there is such an agreement. There should be a backup system to the ASN system. The auditor should ask if this backup system is documented somewhere in the system. If there is to be a rush shipment during an off shift time, then what and who should be contacted in order transfer the ASN. There are firms that provide such services to the supplier(auditee). If the auditee uses such a firm, then check that this firm is on the approved supplier list. This firm provides a valuable service to the auditee.

The glossary reference A.45 defines product as a service. Once the product is distributed to the work areas, the task of inventory control for inprocess/final goods can be covered by the sub element 4.15.3.2. What type of system is used to perform the optimization of the inventory turns? This can be addressed in the Management Review of the analysis of company level data or a continuous improvement project. The standard states about the use of "fifo" and stock rotation. The auditor should ask the opened ended question of what is the prescribed method used. The information is to be reviewed to see of this method meets the intent of the standard. This requires judgment and experience of the auditor. There are many methods to accomplish this requirement. The auditor should be open minded and of a diverse background to review the particular method. Also the particular method to distribute the work to the work areas can be diverse in nature according the product being manufactured. This method to assign work should be documented in the procedures or work instructions for others to follow.

Performance monitoring to 100% on-time delivery to the customer can be done in this function or it is done in the Management Review. In any case, the requirement is to have a system to track on-time delivery to all customers. This is a proactive approach. Many suppliers(auditees) use the customer reports to track on time delivery. This is an incorrect approach. The occurrence of a late delivery or partial delivery is first known by the supplier(auditee). If the supplier waits until the customer sends a monthly report, then it is too late to respond. The standard clearly states that the supplier is to establish systems to support 100% on-time deliveries to meet production and service requirements. Anyone who has worked in the automotive sector knows that this means prompt attention to these releases by the customer. There is an unpardonable cardinal "sin" for shutting down an automotive assembly plant because of a missed shipment. Therefore it follows the customer is to be notified of anticipated delivery problems. Personnel in production control departments know of this requirement. There must be a systematic approach to support the customer's demands. Corrective actions are required to improve the performance of the delivery problem. The auditor should check if these corrective actions follow element 4.14, Corrective and preventive action. There have been occurrences when auditee's have responded by telling an auditor that the customer did not require a corrective action. The standard requires a corrective action. This action should have a cause, corrective action, controls to ensure that the action is effective, and preventive action to ensure that it will not reoccur. Repeat incidents to on-time delivery should be investigated closely. These repeat incidents could constitute a Major nonconformance. This would be a Major due the fact that corrective action is ineffective to satisfy customer requirements. Again, it must be noted that the auditor should look at the corrective actions and the causes to determine if the actions are ineffectual. Customer performance reports are a source of further investigation for on-time delivery. During the Management Review of customer satisfaction, the auditor should note the discrepancies to the delivery ratings. The auditor should investigate these ratings or assign them to another. The auditor should take time to seek out the other auditor and provide this auditor with the information and instructions of what is required.

The audit of this function is to include the tracking of premium freight. This tracking does not necessarily have to be in money denominations, but can be by occurrence. The intent is to have a record of the premium freight. This can be kept by the accounting department. If this is the case, then the auditor is to go to the accounting department to see if this tracking is being performed. It is worthy of note that this is a system audit of all functions involved to support the standard and the policy of the firm being audited. There is no overt reference to the Accounting department in the standard, however this function does provide data for cost of poor quality, scrap, and variances to the budget. These variances lead to measures of efficiency and productivity. The purpose of the author's digression is to bring forth the idea that a cross functional or multidisciplinary team is vital to the success of the implementation of the standard and the business.

X.
Production/Manufacturing/ Process Control

A. Documentation Required:

In performing the audit in the manufacturing area, there are certain documents and records that need to be reviewed before performing this part of the process approach audit. The manufacturing area should be about 60 to 65 % of the audit of the auditee's functions/processes. In order to gain a good perspective of what the auditee requires of its manufacturing process, the auditor is to review the procedure(s) for the way or manner of production is conducted. There are always many different ways to accomplish this requirement. The auditor should not assume that there is only one prescribed method. Read the procedures that are linked to the elements of process control, inspection, identification & trace ability, status of the product, calibration identification of equipment & gages, nonconforming product. All of these procedures or work instructions are closely related to the production, manufacturing/process control processes. The auditor should obtain a facility plan of the plant(s). On this plan the Lead auditor is to diagram the location of where the other auditor(s) and lead auditor are to cover during the audit. This is a helpful aid to the auditee's guides and the auditors in order to not cover duplicate areas and to cover all of the affected manufacturing areas. Next is to obtain the control plans, process FMEAs, and flow charts of the above mentioned areas/part numbers that are to be audited. This gives direction to all involved as to what is the central focus of this part of the audit. Obtain a drawing list or master document list. This will be used before and during the audit to verify that all current versions of drawings are in use. At every area of the audit, there is always an audit of documentation control for the latest versions of all documents.

B. Review:

The review process begins with reading the procedures that pertain to the identification of product throughout the manufacturing process. Make note as to what is done at various stages. If trace ability is required by contract, review the contract for the depth and requirement. Also read as to how the status of the product is identified as to nonconformance or conformance in relationship to the inspections or tests. How does the auditor know, or anyone else, what is good and what is not good in the shop area. Check that there are contingency plans for unforeseen events and who is responsible. What is the method to maintain the plant in a clean condition? Later, during the actual area audit, observe the conditions of the entire area(s). Obtain a facility plan layout of the manufacturing area and mark it up as to the areas to be audited by the lead auditor and auditor(s). This is a valuable item for the guides. They know where the auditors are going and can obtain the proper management personnel to help. The control plans are reviewed prior to the actual audit to see if the revision dates of the part numbers are the same as the control plan. In addition to this, the auditor is to verify that the drawing of the part number has significant characteristics. If the characteristics are on the drawing, then the auditor should check the process FMEA, flow chart, as well as the control plan. While reviewing the drawing, look for specific test requirements that may be referenced on the engineering specifications. The engineering specifications are usually noted within the body of the drawing as notes or in a separate section. The auditor should ask to see the specification and verify that there are any required interval/frequency for such tests. Some customers require an annual layout of all dimensions. This layout is to be denoted on the control plan. The auditor is to note the required raw material or sub components required from the drawing onto the control plan or the checklist. During the on site audit of the manufacturing area, this will serve as a reminder of what is required. It is a good practice to also note what are the trace ability and identification requirements from the review of the above mentioned procedures. The control plan is the main central guide to the manufacturing audit. The PFMEA is to be reviewed in comparison to the control plan for the current controls. The current controls on the FMEA should closely match those of the control plan. In addition, the drawing is to reviewed to the FMEA for any critical or safety characteristics. The safety items are to be denoted on the FMEA and review if there are actions or controls for the high severity of these characteristics. The auditor should first focus on the safety and significant characteristics during the manufacturing audit. These items are of high importance to the auditee and customer.

This introduces another point of the review. The control plan is to describe the reaction or action plan if a condition of out of control or specification is encountered. The auditor is to review this plan with the employees in the manufacturing areas. This is also part of the nonconforming process that was covered in the chapter on Quality.

The review of the above documents is not intended to be a documentation audit that is performed before the initial certification audit. The review is to familiarize the auditor(s) with the auditee's methods of controlling the manufacturing process. It is to be noted that the specification for ISO/TS-16949:1999 does not specify what method to use to fulfill the requirements. In many cases, the auditee will devise innovative techniques to satisfy these requirements. The auditor is to have an open, objective mindset to understand these unique methods and to make an objective judgment onto the effectiveness of the implementation. The auditee has the right to appeal any nonconformance that they feel is not correct. If the auditor has not judged their methods objectively, this appeal is to be submitted to the registrar with evidence.

C. Audit of the Processes for manufacturing.

When beginning the audit of the manufacturing area, look at the general conditions. See if there is an overall orderliness to what is observed. An experienced auditor is usually capable of getting a certain "feel" for these conditions. If there are boxes and equipment all over the areas or no sense of flow of the manufacturing process, then there is a good indication that the housekeeping function is not effective. A cautionary note is inserted here for being too overly enthusiastic to write a nonconformance for cleanliness. The auditor should be astutely aware of the particular business of the auditee. The condition of the area for a foundry or steel mill is vastly different in comparison to an electronics assembly operation. Careful analysis of the overall situation should be used before making a judgment on the satisfactory conditions of housekeeping.

At the first operation that is listed on the control plan, verify that the raw material that is being used is correct to the notes that were taken during the review. Ensure that the material or sub components are identified properly as the auditee has so documented. Also review what or how is the status of the condition of the material is to results of testing or inspection. The notes on the control plan from the previous review should be consulted for the references to the correct material or applicable components. While observing the proper raw material or components, look for a subcontractor name. Make note of the name and verify that this subcontractor is on the approved list or that they are in the system for the purchasing/materiale's department. It is important to note that the verification for the raw material or components is correct to the drawing or specification. There have been many occurrences where this is not correct and the resulting consequences are that of a product recall due to failures in the field.

The particular operation should be in sequence to the flow chart or indented bill of materials from an MRP system. The auditor should verify at every operation that the sequence is correct to that of what was approved by the customer. This approval is by way of the Product Approval Process. This is also known as the sample submission to the customer. If the auditor is in doubt as to the correct sequence, then the auditor should request the sample package and verify that the sequence and correct material subcontractors are as what was approved by the customer. Any deviations from this approved package are to have customer approval. Major nonconformances have been written for failure to notify the customer of any changes. The specification states that the supplier shall obtain prior customer authorization whenever a product or process is different from that which is currently approved. The current approved process is the one that the customer has seen as a sample submission to the requirements of the specific customer. The auditor and the auditee should verify what are the customer specifics for any such changes. The changes also involve any subcontractor too. Check the identification of the raw material or sub components to the required procedure or documentation. Ensure that the proper tags or records are retained for trace ability. This is crucial when auditing to safety products such as brake and steering systems, headlight systems, and airbags. The auditor should know what type of product requires these special requirements.

At each operation of the process, the auditor should ask the operator(s) how do they perform their tasks. Then observe them in the performance and verify these tasks to the appropriate job instruction. Ask for their training or qualifications and make note of their names for the audit in the human resources/training function. If there are no job instructions, then ask how are they qualified to perform the job. There are companies that provide all training to their employees instead of documented job instructions. Job instructions may take the form of any documents that is normally used by the supplier to provide the necessary information. The auditor, should he or she encounter this method, are to take notes of names, operations, and tasks for a later audit in the training function. The training function/process would have to be lengthened in time in order to cover the sampling of the auditor. This is a laborious process, but it has to be done in order to verify the appropriate items. Job instructions are to be at the work station and are to be controlled. Check that they are accessible to the operator. Most of the time if the instructions are in a close proximity, then they are at the work station. If they are across the plant and in the supervisor's desk, then they are not accessible. The auditor is to use their judgment when evaluating this element. When observing the operator performing the work task, look to see if there are tools, fixtures, or gages used and are they included in the job instruction(s). The key item here is that if the particular tool, gage, or the fixture are removed from the operator, can they perform their job. Please note that the job instruction can take on many forms in order to perform the job. The auditor is to thoroughly check for all appropriate documents. There may be more than one particular instruction. Ask if there is a first piece set up approval in effect. Check that this has been performed and if the appropriate approvals have been noted. This is dependent upon the auditee's process and the documentation required. If there is a dedicated operation that never changes, then there might not be a set up. In some organizations, a first piece approval is required for each shift. Check the documentation for appropriateness. If the first piece is retained, then ask to see it checked again in view of the auditor. There have been occasions when this first piece does not conform to the gage or required specification. When this occurs, ask who approved the set up and seek an explanation. There might be an approved deviation from the customer or the auditee's management. With any deviation, ensure that the characteristic is a customer requirement from the drawing or relevant specification. The consequence of an unapproved deviation that effects the customer, is a major nonconformance.

The control plan, as the main reference, is checked that the operator performs the inspection checks at the required frequencies and using the correct equipment/gages. Compare the control plan statements with what is actually being performed. If the operator does more than required, then there is no problem. Review the record of the requirements to see that there is a clear criteria of acceptance and authorization to release. The authorization to release is usually a signature, initials, or clock number on the record. These records can, again, take many different variations in order to accomplish the task. The auditor should review all carefully for effectiveness. During the drawing reviews if there are significant characteristics, then they are to be on the control plan. Review the method in which the auditee controls these items. One approach is the use of statistical process control charts or spc charts. The auditor is to review these charts as a method of statistical techniques. Are the charts in a state of statistical control? The auditor should investigate that any unstable conditions are annotated on the reverse of the chart or other document to show that there was action to these conditions.

Also, there should be notations for tool and material changes annotated on or next to the chart. If there are occurrences of out of control or specification limits, ask the operator what is the reaction plan to these events. Compare the answer to the reaction plan on the control plan. Follow the audit trail of the out of specification points to see how the nonconforming product was dispositioned. There have been times when the process is in a state of control, but there is data that show out of specification. The auditor is to bring that to the attention of the operator and management representative. There is a potential for a major nonconformance due to the fact that no one recognized this occurrence. The reaction is to be used for all events of nonconforming or out of control data. This is an important point for the auditee and auditor. Potential problems to the customer can be avoided.

Make a note of the gages/equipment that is used to perform the tasks of collecting or recording data. Note if they are current for the calibration interval. Of course there does not have to be a visual indicator or "sticker" on the gage. However, there does have to be a suitable indicator. Inquire as to what the auditee uses to indicate this status. Review the procedure or work instruction or policy. The auditor is to make a note on the check sheet to check the record of calibration when auditing the lab or appropriate area where the records are kept. The use of fail-safe devices are a method of comparative references using test software or hardware to judge the quality of the product and to prevent bad parts from getting to the customer. These devices are to be checked periodically and recorded. Verify that they have done so as per the documentation provided to the operator. There have been occasions when the test parts have not detected good or bad parts.

When interviewing the operator(s), ask how they handle a nonconforming part when it is discovered. Listen and observe to what is being said and done, then compare this to the reaction plan within the control plan. Follow this trail to the nonconforming area or documents to see that the nonconforming parts are disposed in the documented manner. Ensure that the reworked parts, if they are reworked, are re-inspected and returned to the production properly. If parts are reworked, verify that there are documented rework instructions for all personnel involved. These details of the rework instructions are dependent upon the product and the detail of the rework. The auditor should use an experienced judgment when reviewing these documents.

Most present operations perform the packaging operations at the last operation of the production sequence. This is common in the injection molding industry when the operation is a "shoot and ship". Ask the operator how are the parts packed and if there are instructions on how to pack them. Verify that the instructions are correct to the actual packaging or to the required customer packaging guidelines. Observe the labels and the bar codes for a revision letter or number referenced to part number. Compare this revision level to the control plan or the drawing. Also compare the correct quantity and protective internal packaging.

As a final question, ask the operator if they have had training in their job or how are they qualified to perform the job. Listen to the reply and make notes to verify in the training area for the proper records or documents. Make a note of the operator's name in order to see their training record later.

The audit of the manufacturing area takes into account many different elements and sections of the standard. It is not only an audit of process control. The auditor is to have a full awareness of the situation in manufacturing. This can only be acquired by experience in this process. This is to be a requirement of all auditors for the particular industry that the auditee in engaged. Without this experience, the audit is nothing but a review of a prepared checklist.

XI.
Maintenance, Tooling, and Facilities Management

The maintenance function is to have planned a preventative maintenance system. This will consist of planned, scheduled, maintenance activities, predictive methods, replacement parts for key equipment, preserving equipment, and improving objectives. The purpose of all of these "Shalls" is to ensure that there is no equipment failure that would prevent the shipment of product to the customer on time. The auditee is to select key equipment to ensure that this purpose is fulfilled for customer satisfaction. The ISO portion of the standard, 4.9.1.1.g, describes this as "...continuing process capability." This portion of the standard is sometimes confused with the concept of process capability in statistical process control. Auditors have seen a great quantity of spc charts and histograms for the use in maintenance. This is incorrect and usually leads the auditor to writing nonconformances for the SPC that is not done correctly. These are unnecessary Ncs. There should be procedures to describe the maintenance activities. The standard does not overtly denote that there are documented procedures, but the ISO portion, 4.9.1.1.a, does say that the absence of such procedures could affect quality. The auditor is to review the procedures to gain an understanding of the system. While performing the audit in manufacturing, the auditor should make note of some of the key equipment encountered.

The auditor is to ask for a schedule of the maintenance of all of the key equipment. This is the "planned activities". The schedule will take the form of many different variations. The auditor should see that there is equipment, dates, tasks, and responsibilities. This can be accomplished by a written 3-ring notebook to a sophisticated integrated software program on a computer. Both are acceptable as long as the objective is accomplished. From this list of equipment, the auditor is to select a random sample or the noted sample from the production audit, and ask to see the required maintenance records. A common question is to ask if there is a preventive maintenance backlog. Be sure to ask for a "preventive" maintenance backlog. Almost all maintenance departments have a backlog of some kind. This is because there are priorities. The effectiveness of the total preventive maintenance system is that all of the scheduled activities have been completed. This also reflects upon the allocation of resources for the function.

Some of the key pieces of equipment in most manufacturing firms are the compressors, main production equipment, cranes and hoists, and forklifts. The auditor should start with these items. Check the required tasks and dates. Also check the past records to see if there is a continuity and consistency to the total maintenance system. The Planned activities are to match the actual. This is similar to a calibration system. The records are kept like an accounting ledger, planned to actual.

The system is to have predictive maintenance. This is the early or planned replacement of certain items within the equipment that are known to fail. Predictive maintenance can also mean the analysis of oils or fluids. The compressors are periodically checked for contaminants in the oil. The oil subcontractor usually provides this service of oil analysis. The report shows what parts of the compressor are eminent for failure. The analysis of the coolant fluids in a machining center can tell when to change the filter or fluid. These checks are sometimes performed by the operator or a technician using a refractometer. The machine fluids check is a process parameter and will be on the control plan. The instrument used is to be calibrated if this function is important. The use of an infrared camera for hot spots in the circuit breaker boxes or buss line is another form of predictive maintenance. This is seen in stamping operations where the vibrations from the presses cause the loosening of bolts and breakers. The review of all of the repair maintenance work orders is used to improve the preventive aspects. The department head, at some interval of time, reviews a prioritized breakdown of the highest number of repair incidents. The changing of the frequency of the tasks is a result of the review. These are but a few of ideas for maintenance.

The department is to have availability of replacement parts. This could be an in-house inventory. Check that such an inventory exists. During the manufacturing audit, make note of the types of key equipment used. The replacement parts should contain the most frequent parts that wear out or break down. Ask if there is an analysis of all of the repairs performed. See if there is a common thread of replaced parts. Are these parts in the inventory for replacements. If there is an inventory kept with records, then the auditor should sample some of the areas and see if the parts are really included on the inventory list or computer. In all cases, make sure that the replacement parts exist. If there are parts that are purchased, ensure that they are either local or have a short time in transit. The intent here is not to have a piece of equipment down so that shipments are missed to the customer.

Packaging and preservation of equipment, tooling, and gauging is a frequent item that is missed by the auditee and auditor. The preservation and packaging of equipment are to protect from environmental harm. Many times a company will "mothball" a piece or an entire line of equipment for a certain length of time. When a new order arrives to produce a product, it is discovered that the equipment is not in a condition to perform quickly. The result is a late delivery or nonconforming product. Gauging can also be critical to the measurement process. Test equipment or gages that are serviced or calibrated by an outside source need to be packaged properly to prevent damage. The result is the same as for the equipment if the test equipment or gage is damaged upon arrival at the calibration or servicing source. What most auditees miss in this requirement is the return to the auditee. Does the auditee communicate to the servicing source how to package the equipment for the return? These same analogies are also applied to the tooling that may be outsourced or stored.

After all of the above has been reviewed, the next item is the documenting, evaluating, and improving of maintenance objectives. These objectives may be covered in the management review of Quality system performance or Analysis and use of company level data. The objectives for maintenance need to be documented in some sort of form. The auditor is to ask for objective evidence of these objectives. Once the objectives have been established, then see if they have been evaluated. The collection of data without action or a comment is worthless. The idea of the objectives is to improve these objectives. This is the same as the objectives for company level data. There should be a goal, target, benchmark, or trend for the objectives. This can take the form of machine uptime, downtime, or readiness. Some other forms are the completion of all of the maintenance tasks on time. Another form is the quantity of repair work orders or occurrences. The repairs for the year or the quarter are to be lowered by 10%. This is measured by the amount of man-hours expended. This is a form of labor variance as to the budget. The improvement of the objectives can be in the Continuous Improvement program that the firm has adopted. The bottom line is that the objectives must be documented, evaluated, and improved.

Depending upon the type of company that is being audited, tool management may be an area to be audited or it may be under subcontractor evaluation. The in house customer tools are to be identified as to ownership. This can be done in many ways. The most common is a number designation located directly on the tool. This number designation is directly traceable to ownership in the accounting records as a plant asset or customer asset. The auditor should take a sampling of various tool numbers and trace them back to discover the ownership. Other times, the markings are very obvious such as the customer name and part number. These tools are to have a tool management program similar to the maintenance program. The program should show the care and periodic maintenance of these tools. This is usually the case in the areas of metal stamping, molding, roll forming, fabric cutting, and die casting. The tools are to be in a program much like the equipment for preventive maintenance. The supplier(auditee) is to provide resources to maintain these tools in working order. If the tool life has been exceeded, then it is up to the auditee(supplier) to notify the purchasing authority of this condition. This is a change of a new tool to replace old tooling. A production part approval is to be submitted to the customer. These items should be investigated by the auditor as audit trails to follow. The personnel performing the tool maintenance are to be qualified. The auditor should check what are the qualifications of the tool room personnel. This can be done when auditing the Human Resource or Training function.

Perishable tools are used mostly in the machining operations, but can also have an application in stamping, die cutting of materials, wood cutting operations, and any operation where the tool can be sharpened. The idea of sharpening of a tool can be expensive to the auditee. In some cases, the method of tool management is to discard the tool and buy new. It is more cost effective. The auditor should look carefully at the whole operation to determine the effectiveness of the program. In the case of machining operations, the operator or technician changes multiple tools at a predetermined frequency. The frequency is determined by tool life studies or recommendations from the tool supplier. These tool changes are recorded in a log or on control charts. These tools are then submitted to the tool shop or maintenance department for sharpening. Resources are needed to properly sharpen the tools. The auditor is to check that these resources are present. Sometimes these tools are sent to an outside source. Verify that the source is on the approved subcontractor list or is on file in the purchasing department.

The sources that build the tools are to be tracked for completion. This is performed in the Product Realization phase that was discussed in a previous chapter. If there are replacement tools or extra tools being made, the auditor should verify that there is a production part approval or notification to the customer purchasing authority of these facts.

Facility and equipment planning are discussed during the product realization process. Methods for effective operations, lean manufacturing events, time studies, and ergonomics are items to be found in the continuous improvement program. During the management audit interview, the auditor should ask to see that these items are being addressed. There needs to be objective evidence to show compliance.

In all, the maintenance and tooling programs follow a program of timed response. The timing is pre-planned through the use of experience or manufacture's recommendations. The proof that these programs are being performed in the timely manner is the records that are retained.

XII.
Laboratories

The subelement 4.10.6 states that the supplier's laboratory is required to comply to ISO/IEC-17025 including the use of a laboratory scope. The audit of the laboratories, if more than one, needs to be evaluated to the above mentioned specification. Compliance to this requirement will include all of the shalls in the 17025 standard. Looking at the standard, this appears to be imposing. However, if one sees that many of the required "shalls" are actually covered in the TS-16949 standard and the QS-9000 standard. External testing and calibration sources are required to be accredited to ISO/IEC-17025. This means that any testing or calibration performed by the outside source is to have a certificate showing the certification. Along with this certification, there should also be a scope of the tests or calibrations that it, the laboratory, has the competence to perform.

There are some definitions that need clarification. An accredited laboratory is one that has been reviewed and approved by a nationally recognized accreditation body. This is in the glossary as A.1. A nationally recognized body would be the A2LA, SCC, CoFRAC, or a list generated by the country of origin. The auditor would have to be familiar with this list as well as the auditee. A laboratory scope is a quality record that includes specific tests and calibrations performed, the list of equipment it uses to perform the tests, and a list of methods & standards to which it performs these tests and calibrations. This is usually a one page record listing the required three items in a columnar format. The auditor is to have a copy of this scope at the beginning if the audit. The most common nonconformances for the lab scope is that it does not include the calibrations that a company performs. Many auditees confuse the fact that there does not have to be a separate location to be called a laboratory. Calibration is defined, in glossary A.7, as a the relationship of values indicated as compared to values to a reference standard. This definition is confused with a common definition that calibration includes the adjustment, repair, and maintenance of equipment and gages. This is very common in the machining and stamping industries. Another common NC is that the outside sources are not accredited to ISO\IEC-17025 or GUIDE-

25. Auditees often confuse the accreditation to ISO-9001/2 with 17025 or GUIDE-25. The certificates from the outsourced test or calibration labs only state the ISO-9001 or 9002 certification. This is not correct to the standard. Along with this nonconformance, the scope of the laboratory is not complete to the required test or calibration. An example of this is an outsourced laboratory that conducts a test for radiographic analysis for voids in a casting. However the laboratory scope shows that this laboratory is not certified to perform this particular test. There is a select group of organizations that are capable to certify outside laboratories. They are required to provide a certificate and a scope of what the laboratory is capable to perform in the way of tests or calibrations. The auditee and the auditor are to verify that these laboratories have the proper certificates and scopes. The auditor should ensure that the certificates received or reviewed are from a source that is certified to ISO/IEC-58. There may be sources that grant certificates that are not accredited to the above mentioned standard. It is up to the auditee to check that the accreditation body is accredited to this ISO standard.

The contents of ISO/IEC-17025 contain many sections and mandatory "shalls" that are required in order to comply. This standard was written with the intent that outside, commercial, laboratories would be certified. The use of this standard to laboratories within the auditee's organization applies to only certain sections of the standard. Many sections of the standard are covered by ISO/TS-16949. It is up to the auditor and auditee to verify which of these sections do and do not apply. The following will cover the two (2) pertinent sections of the standard. Management, 4.0, will require that the laboratories have procedures for testing and calibration as well as describing the responsibilities of the personnel who work in the laboratory. This is usually done in the documentation phase of element 4.1. The procedures will normally be in the lab or in a separate lab manual. These procedures are to document controlled as all procedures. The other section pertains to tests or calibrations that are outsourced to subcontractors. These tests and/or calibrations that are sourced outside are to be to competent laboratories. This means that the outsourced labs also are to be accredited to ISO/IEC-17025. A common nonconformance is that these labs are not accredited. The exact terminology is that the outsourced laboratories comply with this international standard.

The technical section has to do with personnel, environmental conditions, test & calibration methods, nonstandard methods, uncertainty, maintenance, and traceability. Personnel are to competent to operate the equipment. This is audited in the Human Resource or Training function. The personnel are to be qualified based upon education, training, or experience. The auditor is to select names of the laboratory personnel and confirm that qualifications are established and there are records or evidence that the appropriate personnel meet these qualifications. It is important to note that the personnel should have practical and theoretical knowledge. Some of this evidence is certificates of training, college courses, and subcontractor(auditee) training. A requirement of the 17025 standard which is not required under 16949, is that the laboratory keep current job descriptions of managerial and technical personnel. This paragraph becomes a dilemma for the auditor. In most firms there are job descriptions in use. When this is not the case, then there is the conflict between the ISO/TS-16949 and ISO/IEC-17025 standards. The auditor should write the nonconformance if there are no job descriptions. IF there is a complaint from the auditee, then the auditor should inform them of the appeals process. The appeals process is required for all registrars.

Control of the environmental conditions of the laboratory are required when it is necessary by the test or specifications in use. Some tests required a normalizing of the samples for 24 hours before testing in a controlled atmosphere. These conditions are stated in the test method. The auditor and auditee are to read the test method or specification to verify that any such conditions exist. The monitoring of such conditions is to be done using equipment that is certified and calibrated. This is a common nonconformance that the instruments used to measure the environment, thermometers and barometers, have not been calibrated or are not in the calibration system. The auditor is to be sure that the control of the laboratory conditions is justified either by the required specification or documented in the auditee's procedures. Another common nonconformance is that the auditee documents that the laboratory will be controlled to a temperature with an assigned tolerance. Upon performing the audit, the auditor discovers that this is not being done or the temperature is out of range of the tolerance and there is no action or notation.

The methods and specifications used in the laboratory are documented in the scope. All of these documents are to be on site in the laboratory. The media can be hard copy or electronic. The auditor is to verify that the correct revision level is being used. This is done by comparing these documents to the master list or equivalent. These methods are to include calibration as well as tests. Laboratory scope nonconformances have been written because the calibration method has not been included or documented. Essentially, these methods are work instructions that describe how to calibrate micrometers, calipers, etc. More sophisticated pieces of equipment are to have these "work instructions". The methods that are standardized are usually easy to document through subscription services or CD-ROMs. The nonstandard methods are harder since they are commonly created by the laboratory personnel. These methods are to be validated. There are various techniques to the validation. Some of these are listed in the ISO/IEC-17025 standard. It is also required that records of these validation are available and a procedure for the validation. The uncertainty of all measurements of calibrations is also required as well as a procedure. This requirement parallels the ISO/TS-16949 standard in subelement 4.11.1.1, which is also an ISO requirement. The level of uncertainty and the calculation is not a simple event. It is suggested that the auditor and auditee refer to note 3 of the 17025 standard which refers to ISO-5725. In a previous note, there is a guidance that the degree of rigor is dependent upon many factors. Before the auditor writes a nonconformance, it would be wise to carefully view all of the evidence on uncertainty and the auditee's explanation and the procedure.

Records of tests and calibrations are the same as the TS standard with the exception that there is to be a maintenance plan for the equipment. This would be for extensive equipment that requires such maintenance. The auditee should consult the manual(s) that came with the equipment to determine what maintenance is required. A procedure is also required for the handling, storage, and planned maintenance of the equipment. This is in addition to the required procedures of the TS standard.

Traceability to an international or national standard is a requirement for QS-9000. This standard, TS-16949 and ISO/IEC-17025, require traceability to International Units (SI). The auditor and the auditee will have difficulty in verifying that the standards used are traceable to these SI units. There are some organizations that do not what are the SI units. It should be sufficient to verify that the standards are traceable to the national or international standard.

The technique of auditing the laboratory is to obtain the laboratory scope and to ask to see a select sampling of all of the methods and standards. The auditor verifies that they are present and under documentation control. Calibrations are determined by using the identification numbers of the gages and/or equipment obtained during the manufacturing or engineering audits. During these audits, the auditor should note the identification number of these various gages or equipment on the checksheet. It is a good practice to note these items in the section 4.11. Then when the audit of the lab takes place, the auditor has a representative sample of items used to measure or develop product for the customer. The routine is to ask the appropriate auditee for the records of tests or calibrations. Calibration records should contain location, frequency, date of calibration, type of equipment, check method, due date of next calibration, remarks as to damage, condition when received and completed, and acceptance criteria(tolerance of checks). An important note for auditors is to check that the checks made are within the tolerance range(acceptance criteria). This level of detail during the audit is warranted to determine if the auditee is reviewing such records periodically. Nonconformances have been written when outsourced gage blocks have a record that shows that one or many of the gage blocks are out of tolerance to the prescribed grade. These records also are to reviewed by the auditee. All calibrations are to be traceable. Ask the auditee what is the standard used to calibrate and for the certificate or record of the standard. Remember, all outsourced calibration sources are to be certified to ISO/IEC-17025. The auditor should ask for the certificates of these sources and ensure that they are approved subcontractors.

Test failures in laboratories are to have corrective actions to the disciplined problem solving method described in element 4.14. The auditor is to investigate these failures for compliance to affected standards from the customer. Certain customer tests that are performed on an annual or periodic basis, require the auditee to immediately shut down production and notify the customer. When reviewing the test record failure, find out what specification is requiring this test. Obtain the specification and read it with the auditee to verify if the above condition is mandated. Failure to notify the customer and quarantine affected product is a Major nonconformance.

In all, the laboratory is to viewed as to condition of the equipment, records of compliance to tests and calibrations, reactions to failures, and traceability to accepted standards. It is suggested that the auditor have experience in working in a laboratory in order to perform the audit.

XIII.
Human Resources/Training

The purpose of this function as related to the audit is the verification of appropriate training and qualifications of all personnel within the organization. The particular function may vary amongst various companies depending upon the size of the organization. In large ones there is a separate function for human resources and training. Smaller firms will have multiple personnel assuming this function as well as others. The main result is the training of all personnel for the implementation and continuous improvement of the organization. Personnel are to be trained or qualified for their particular job or function. It is the responsibility of the management function to provide this training or qualified personnel for each function.

The primary function of this element is the assessment of training needs within the organization. The procedures for this element shall describe the assessment of training needs. The auditor is to read this procedure to see what are the assessed needs for training and an appropriate training plan. Many small organizations do not assess these needs and do not have an appropriate training plan. This is a most important aspect of the standard. Without further training to enhance the organization, the personnel within are not aware of the current progress of new ideas. This cannot be overemphasized. Once the auditor has this needs assessment, then the task is to verify what items have been completed for the respective training. A cautionary note is that some firms compile a large list of training programs only to not complete most of them. This is common in small firms who have an idealistic view of the training and do not have budgetary approval to implement the training. The level of training is to proceed from the top of the organizational chart to the bottom and to all hourly personnel. Records of training are the evidence that there is completion. There are times that an auditor will view these records only to have them be false. The only evidence an auditor can verify is the record that an event has occurred. It is a very easy task to create or invent records of completed training or any other records. The auditor is left with no resort but to accept these records on good faith. To disprove that these records are false, would have to be that the training is not effective. This can be very difficult. If statistical training has been performed for all manufacturing personnel, then the auditor would have to question most of these people to see if they have an understanding of the statistics. There is always the constraint of time to perform the audit.

Using the organizational chart, the auditor asks to see the qualifications of all of the personnel on the chart. Start with the highest person on the chart. The standard does not require job descriptions, but many firms do have job descriptions. The descriptions should have qualifications for the incumbent. The auditor is to ask to see these descriptions and to verify that there are qualifications on the job descriptions. The next item is to see if the particular personnel actually have the majority of the qualifications to fill these positions. There should be objective evidence.

Senior management are to have training in ISO/TS standards. Ask to see the training records of all of the senior management. The training is usually an executive overview. As one proceeds down the chart, the training becomes more detailed and longer. The most important person for training is the management representative. This person should have the most extensive training. The other persons that are key to having associated training are engineering, laboratory, tooling, maintenance. Engineering personnel should have required training or skills that include CAD/CAM, FMEAs, GD&T, and Reliability. This training could be derived from the training needs assessment by the company or from a previous employer or education. The auditor should select the engineering group designers and the engineering manager to verify training records or past experience. This is not a random selection, but a purposeful one. If the company is design responsible, then this is a very important part of the audit to verify the qualifications and skills. The Tooling department is another key area. If the company is tool oriented manufacturing, then the personnel who build or maintain the tools play a vital role. The qualifications of tool makers or tool repair people can be varied according to the job they perform. The auditee is to define the qualifications either in a job description or some other means. The only standard requires that people performing assigned tasks shall be qualified on the basis of education, training, and/or experience. Tool making or repair people can have a journeyman's card or internal training or years of experience. The key to the qualifications is the specified requirements that the auditee documents. The auditor is to seek the verification to see that all tool personnel fulfill these documented requirements. The effectiveness of these specified qualifications would be objective evidence that the particular personnel cause customer complaints or internal problems where tools are not maintained or repaired properly. This task of proving with objective evidence is difficult. This is also true for any qualification of any person within the organization. The auditor must remember that it is the auditee's requirements that must be audited, not the personal ideas of the auditor. This is an objective audit relying on facts and evidence.

Laboratory personnel are another key group. The people in the lab are to be competent to the requirements of the work in the lab. These qualifications again are documented by the auditee. The auditor should be verifying that these people have practical as well as theoretical training or experience. The training can be internal of by outside sources. Personnel responsible for calibration are to have training as well. There should be certificates or training records for these people to substantiate there credence. The auditor should review the lab scope and see if there are exceptional tests that require exceptional people. Make notes to review these qualifications and records. The lab personnel might have previous training at a a previous employer or at school. The auditor is to verify that these records are in place as well as the auditee. If the training is performed within the organization, the auditor is to verify the credentials of the person conducting the training and the content of the training. There have been occurrences when the person performing the training does not have the background. The content of the training is to be viewed to see what is the extent. One such occurrence was the training of statistical process control where there was no mention of what to do if a process was out of control. When auditing the manufacturing area and if the auditor finds repeated problems of the use of SPC, then a note should be made to check the training records and the content. The effectiveness of the training evaluation should also be scrutinized.

The evaluation of training effectiveness is performed in many ways by auditee. There is no one suggested method as long as the intent is to see the value of the training for the company. If money, time, materials, and human resources are being expended, then management expects a return on the investment. This simple approach is taken in the language that management understands, money. There have been a great many programs to help every quality system to "get better something" but have not addressed the return on the investment. These programs fail because when it comes time to reconcile the costs, there is no benefit to the bottom line. In order to "sell" management on the "program du jour", one must show how money will be saved or revenues increased. The training program from the needs assessment should move with this objective in mind. In this way the program will get the attention and acceptance by upper management. The evaluation of training effectiveness should track the savings or increase in revenue form the training. The audit of the effectiveness can be by way of tests, surveys, actual observation, or performance reviews. All of these will have to be reduced down to the idea of money. The use of SPC is of value if processes are discovered to cause unnecessary variation that also causes repair or rework within the plant. It is of no value if there are just charts with meaningless data that are filed and forgotten. Operators or inspectors that perform the SPC correctly are only doing what they were instructed to do. This is only a cursory evaluation of the intent of the training and the money spent. To get the real value from the training, a goal must be used to enhance the financial well being of the firm.

As was pointed out in the management chapter, there is a requirement for the measurement of employee motivation, empowerment, and satisfaction. The primary intent of this subelement is for the understanding of the quality objectives that the company sets for all employees. The motivation part will be difficult. Most management people know that people must motivate themselves and rarely can be motivated by being sent slogans or didactic lectures. However, with the intent of knowing if employees understand the objectives of quality and of the consequences of nonconformity of the quality standards there is usually a survey sent out by the Human Resource department to all employees. These surveys are returned and tabulated for information to the management team. The auditor is to verify that there is a measurement technique in place, it encompasses all of the items of the standard, and that it is sent to all employees. Even senior management people are not exempt and should be of the highest importance. What is done with all of the data collected? As in the management chapter, the use of the data is valuable only if it can be related to the efficiency of the company. What are the consequences of customer non conformities to the welfare of the continuation of the business and continuous employment? This question is more in line with economic consequences and can be related to all personnel. It affects everyone's welfare of their life. The auditor should ask if there is a use for the data or it just being performed to satisfy the standard and the auditor. The rhetorical question is "Are we using the survey data as a cost avoidance or a nonconformance avoidance?".

The standard asks if there are resources for trained personnel for internal auditors. The auditee should define the requirements for internal auditors somewhere in the documented quality system. As with other jobs, there needs to be qualifications for the internal auditors. The auditor is to verify that the required training or qualifications are in the training record of all individuals that are internal auditors. A cautionary note to the auditee is that there are some customer specifics that the required training and experience for internal auditors. The auditor and the auditee must know these customer specifics and the auditee has to provide records that the personnel comply.

Common nonconformances are that senior management personnel do not have qualifications specified or no training in ISO/QS-9000, qualifications for lab or technical personnel are not specified, required training is not done or there is no record, and new employees have not been trained to perform the assigned jobs.

The audit of the Human Resource/Training function might have to cover many sections or people if there is a large organization. In smaller companies, this function might be done by the manufacturing or quality manager. The auditor should allow for the time to effectively audit this function.

XIV.
Information Technology/M IS/ Data Systems

The function to be audited is a combination of many functions that deal with the handling of data through the use of computers and other "rapid system collectors/dispensers of information". This is commonly called the "data system function" or the "computer guys", to use a slang expression. This chapter will also cover the retention of all records required by the standard, regulatory standards, and others deemed necessary by the auditee's organization.

The protection of these records is vital to the auditee and the auditor. The records are the proof to the implemented policies and procedures. The protection of these records are important to the audit as well as any regulatory requirements. When auditing the data processing department the auditor is to ask how these records or data are assured of retention and retrieval. This is par to the procedure under collection, accessing, and filing. Of course if the auditee does not use a computer based system, then the procedure is one of manual storage, protection, and file maintenance. In any case there is to be a documented procedure or a paragraph to one main procedure. Protection is usually performed by someone in the data processing function or a person assuming this responsibility. The auditor is to verify that there is a procedure and to see how past records are retrieved on a timely basis. There should be a work instruction or part of a procedure that describes how often the records are backed up and where they are stored for protection. The auditor is to verify that the protection is sufficient. This is a judgment call based on the actual observation. In most cases, that auditee has a safe or a media proof box or off site facility. Again, the auditor is to make the judgment on the appropriateness of the storage vehicle.

The element 4.16 requires <u>documented procedures</u> for the identification, collection, indexing, access, filing, storage, maintenance, and disposition of records. Many times during an audit, the auditee has an extraordinarily difficult time locating records. The auditor should ask to see the procedure to determine how these particular records are filed and maintained. This is vital if the records pertain to a critical, safety item or characteristic. If this a "stall" tactic by the auditee then the records will be produced in a short amount of time. This has actually been done in some audits with difficult auditees. Along these same lines, there should be a clause or paragraph describing the timeliness of disposal of these records. The auditor is to verify that they have been disposed. The procedure is to define the retention time and disposal.

Pertinent subcontractor records are a part of this element. The proof of these records extends to other subelements of the standard. If the auditee is not performing receiving inspection, then there should be records of the subcontractor(s)'s performance to previous inspections. Also if there have been corrective actions from subcontractors, it would be wise to retain these as proof that corrective actions have been implemented. Sample submission records are another item that should be retained to show proof that all items on the customer design record(drawing) have been met. These are some of the pertinent records, but others are at the discretion of the auditee. Keep in mind that there is to be a disposal and there are certain customer and regulatory requirements that will come into play. At present there are defined retention periods by major car manufacturers for certain records. These are listed in the customer specifics documents.

The minimum records to be retained, with exception to customer specifics, are listed throughout the standard by a (see 4.16). The standard lists many references to records, when the parenthetical item, (see 4.16), is used then it is to be a retained record. The retention times are also to be listed in the required procedure or work instruction. The following is the list of "(see 4.16)" records in the standard.

quality	4.2.3.1 h
Process verification	4.2.4.9.4
Contract review	4.3.4
Design review	4.4.6
Design verification	4.4.7
Design validation	4.4.8.2
Change implementation	4.5.2.2
Acceptable subcontractors	4.6.2.1

Damaged customer product	4.7.1
Traceability identification	4.8
Qualified processes, equipment, & personnel	4.9.1.1
Control chart process events	4.9.3
Urgent release	4.10.2.3
Inspection and test	4.10.5
Comparative reference checks	4.11.1.1
Calibration records	4.11.2 e
Calibration records+	4.11.3
Repair to nonconforming product	4.13.2
Investigation of cause	4.14.2.1
Internal audit	4.17.1
Follow up to internal audit	4.17.1
training	4.18.1
Management review	4.1.3.1

XV.
Quality

The first word of this standard as well as ISO-9001 and QS-9000 is "Quality". This has in the minds of the writers that it pertains to systems to support the quality of the organization. In the minds of all of those who have worked or are working in Quality departments, it connotes the department of Quality Assurance or Quality Control. Many managers in other departments also have this same connotation in their mind set. On the surface, all of those managers of other departments will fully testify that "Quality is everyone's responsibility". In reality the burden of most of the requirements for these standards rests upon the Quality Manager and the associates in the department. In a time span of seven (7) years of auditing and an approximate total of more than 700 audits, the informal results bear this previous sentence correct. The word "Quality Systems" is synominous with "Quality Department"

Historically, companies have had some sort of a quality department since the time of the industrial revolution. Primarily, the functions and duties of this department were to act as an overseer/policeman of the production personnel and suppliers. In recent times, since the end of World War II, this department has acquired more sophisticated tools and responsibilities. This has not altered the basic premise of the function, that of being enforcer/policeman. This leads one to believe that the Quality function is the "adult/parent" and the manufacturing department as the "adolescent/child". The day-to-day scenario is such as the parent admonishing the child for not performing well in the arena of business. The cause of this strange relationship has as a possible source of the absolving of manufacturing, engineering, purchasing, production control, human resources, and sales functions from their responsibilities and accountabilities. All of the functions that a Quality department performs are really parts of essential, value added functions of a firm. What then do we do about exterminating this Quality function and put "Quality" back to where it belongs?

All of the functions of a Quality department are non-value added in nature. It is composed of a group of indirect labor personnel. However, all of the tools and precepts used are value added. Who then will perform for the quality of the firm? The following is a list of areas/functions/departments that will absorb the Quality department. It is not comprehensive, but only serves as a guideline framework.

Purchasing; Control of all suppliers and subcontractors. Responsible for surveys before and during the business award process. Control of the submission process from these suppliers and their ongoing evaluation and corrective actions. There should be at least one engineer assigned to this department to set and review all drawings and specifications pertaining to the received input to the business.

Accounting; Control of all costs related to the business environment. Provides data and information to Engineering and Production on the following. A. Scrap costs, internal failures, and rework costs. B. Warranty costs, returned goods, customer plant cost recoveries, and external failures. C. Appraisal costs, all areas where an evaluation is made to an established product or process. D. Prevention costs, all areas where use is made of a preventive nature. Costs to review contracts, advanced product meetings, and time to prepare plans of control such as F.M.E.A.s. Accounting should track the investment of all continuous improvement programs for the return on investment.

Sales; The external liaison to the customer. Responsible for the information to Engineering and Production as to customer requirements. Sales handles all customer inquiries such as quotes, complaints, and responds with formal written answers. All drawings, specifications, and other customer requirements emanate from here to the firm. Setting of price and providing of guidelines for manufacturing costs.

Production; Responsible for cost containment and housekeeping of the manufacturing areas. Performs all functions to assure that the product satisfies the customer's requirements by directing the labor force, maintain tools and equipment, testing and inspection of process and product parameters, ongoing product validation, calibration of all gages and test equipment, and process control of all associated processes both tangible and intangible.

Production Control; Responsible for receiving, inprocess, and shipping of the product, pilot runs, nonconforming product control, traceability identifiers, packaging, labeling, for shipped and received product and services.

Engineering; Responsible for planning, designing, construction, management, of all products, processes, equipment, gages, test equipment, floor space, and buildings. The various disciplines are design, product, manufacturing, industrial, environmental, and test engineers. Engineering is also responsible for drawing and specification control, sample submissions, parameter design of processes, reliability and functional testing, and record retention of all tests.

Management; The coordinating of leadership and vision for constancy of purpose. This involves planning, leading, organizing, and controlling of the firm. Some of the main objectives are elimination of fear, barriers, and creation of educational programs for the advancement of the firm and its people. Only the top management personnel can effect changes to make the organization improve on a continuous basis. The Management personnel are the agents of change through benchmarking the organization to similar ones. To greatly enhance the continual improvement process, one has to be a visionary. Therefore the goals and objectives of the organization are to be far reaching to dominance in the propitious niche the organization has chosen.

The Quality department almost always is the caretaker for all corrective actions. The auditor is to read the documented procedure and determine if there are certain items that are out the ordinary from the basic requirements. Key items to look for are a specific time for closure/completion, what type of disciplined problem solving method, specific approvals from management, periodic reports to management, or follow up requirements. When a customer or internal complaint relates in a non compliant product or process, who is promptly informed of these deviations? The person or function should be documented somewhere in the auditee's system. All of the above are not specifically required by the standard, but may be documented in the auditee's procedure(s) as part of the organization's documented quality system. The auditee usually keeps an up to date log of all of the corrective actions on a data base or handwritten system. If this is not the case then the auditor will have to review all of the actions on some sort of a file or notebook. The purpose of this review is to locate the oldest open corrective action. The auditor is to look for the customer complaints first, then the internal corrective actions second. When locating the oldest open corrective action from any customer, also review the customer reports that the auditee has received from that customer. Ensure that the data of both match up correctly. If the auditee has only 3 complaints in the file and the customer report states there are 8, ask and investigate the discrepancy. Check the corrective actions for closure to the procedure or any other requirements. Why are the actions open for a long time. There are occurrences when a corrective action is open for a long time due to involvement with the customer or waiting for a tool to be repaired or for a new gage or new training. This is reasonable providing that there is a temporary actions to protect the customer from a repeat complaint. The auditor should review all of the customer complaints to look for a pattern of repeat occurrences. If there is a pattern of repeat complaints for the same part number or problem, investigate the corrective action of each of these starting with the first occurrence. Read the entire action and make notes. Review the rest of these repeats in chronological order. The purpose is to audit for the effectiveness of the corrective action to eliminate the cause and the problem. If the pattern of occurrences is the same, then the effectiveness of the corrective action is nonconforming. The seriousness with the customer would warrant a major nonconformance. One of the frequent nonconformance in this area is the investigation of the root cause of the problem. This is to be documented in the record of the corrective action. Many times this cause is not investigated or documented that it was investigated. The auditor is the review the corrective action to verify that the cause was eliminated. This is the verification phase. It is to assure that the corrective action is effective and that the controls installed are working. The auditor is to verify a generous sample of all of the corrective actions both internal and external to obtain a decision on the effectiveness of this process. This is an overlooked area of the audit process.

The auditor is to select some of the results of the corrective actions and verify the changes to documentation, or the mistake proofing devices, or additional inspection are in place. The auditor actually goes into the manufacturing or any other area and personally verifies the existence of the actions.

S.P.C. Indices that are below the required 1.33 CpK are to have a corrective action plan with timing and responsibilities. This is another area of the process of corrective action to be verified. The auditor should actually verify that the product is being sorted 100% if the plan has not been completed or to see records of the results of the sort. The plan is to have timing, responsibilities, and objectives to achieve the required 1.33 CpK. This plan is to be readily available to the auditor. The auditee is to show that the process is stable and capable. This means that the control charts are in a state of statistical control before calculating the capability of the process characteristic. This is a frequently overlooked item during the audit by the auditor. All designated characteristics that are on the customer's design record(drawing) are to show compliance to this requirement. The auditee is responsible to show that they are in compliance.

The internal audit is the most valuable tool to the auditee to examine the system. This tool is the inward introspection of the organization to verify that the system is effective and operating correctly to the prescribed controls initiated. Read the procedure for internal auditing. Note special phrases or clauses for planning and implementing the audit. See if there is a section for actually planning of the audit and what are the components required for this planning. Also note the required training for the internal auditors. Make note of this requirement and of the names of the auditors for investigation in the Training/Human resources function. Verify all of the names and there records of training. This is an important item for the audit. If personnel are not qualified for the audit, then there is a good probability that the internal audit will not be effective.

There is to be a schedule describing the timing of the internal audit. The schedule is to be adhered to by the proposed dates itemized. If they have not, this is a nonconformance for not following the plan. The schedule is to modified for customer complaints. Check if there have been customer complaints and has the schedule been modified for those areas that have caused the complaints. These can be a type of "mini" audit of the area(s) affected. The Internal is to be completed and closed out before the external audit is conducted. Completed and closed out means all nonconformances have been closed and Management has reviewed the results in the management review record. If this has not been done, this is a Major nonconformance. If the auditee has not reviewed the system, how can they be prepared for the initial certification audit. One of the first items that has to be provided to the certification body registrar is the results from the internal audit and management review. This is to be verified by the lead auditor in making the judgment for readiness to initiate the audit.

ISO/TS-16949 requires that there be three types of audits for the internal audit. The first is the system audit which is the same type of audit a third party independent auditor would conduct. It is an audit of the entire system for compliance to the technical specification and it is to be to an annual plan. The process audit is the review of the tangible and intangible processes of the organization. The intangible processes are the ones used to support the system. One of these processes is product realization. The purpose of this audit is to reveal how the process is advancing to meet the customer(s) needs to support the vehicle launch. The third type of internal audit is the product audit. This audit verifies that the particular product characteristics are conforming to the customer or auditee's requirements. This is a check that all of the measured items are to print. In all cases the internal auditors are to be independent of the function or process that they audit. This means that if there are auditors that in the normal course of their duties check product, then these auditors are not independent of that process/function.

All activities and functions are to be audited. The auditor is to verify that all of these have been done. This also includes all shifts of operation and weekend shifts. There must be verifiable evidence that all of these shifts have been covered. The activities that are also included are those of the customer specifics and certain auditee specific requirements. These are often missed by the auditee and the auditor during the review of the internal audit process.

The results of these audits are to be reviewed for the corrective actions and the follow ups. A nonconformance is to be written if there is a discrepancy found during the audit. The management personnel of the departments or areas are to take prompt or timely corrective action for these discrepancies. The auditor is to verify who is the management personnel to take the action. Ask the person who is presenting the internal audit what is the responsibility of the issued person of the nonconformance. Ensure that these personnel are management people. This is important from the viewpoint that only the management people will have the authority to carry out the corrective actions to successful completion. Review the actual nonconformances and the corrective actions for adherence to the element on corrective action and to the disciplined problem solving method used by the auditee. Are the corrective actions timely in response? This is an ambiguous phrase within the standard both for ISO and for TS. The auditee is to define what is timely. This phrase begs to be defined by the fact of how it is written. The auditor should ask the auditee how is this defined. It can be done within the internal audit procedure or on the nonconformance. There can be a specified amount of time required in the procedure or date to be closed noted on the nonconformance. In any case, there needs to be a time frame to be closed. The auditor should view the time frame as to credibility. If there is an unusual amount of time to close, then the auditor should tell the auditee that this does not meet the intent of the standard of timely. The auditor is to have experience in this area before declaring this fact to the auditee.

Follow ups to the corrective actions are to be recorded to show the implementation and effectiveness of the closed corrective action. Verify that there has been a record of implementation. The auditor should pick a sample of these follow ups and personally verify them in practice during any of the subsequent areas affected. This will confirm that the corrective actions have taken place. There have been occasions when these follow ups have not taken place as designated on the corrective action. This is an important process for the auditee as it is the introspection of their system.

The effectiveness of the auditee's implementation of the internal audit process is reflected, in part, to the auditor's external audit. If the external auditor discovers an overwhelming amount of nonconformances as compared to the internal audit(s), then the effectiveness of the auditee's process of auditing is deficient. The auditor is to write a nonconformance to this fact. It is the obligation of the auditor to write this nonconformance so that in the future surveillance audits that this does not occur and to inform the auditee to improve their process of auditing.

Most of the time the process of control and recording of the nonconforming process is also performed by the Quality function. There is usually adjunct help from the manufacturing or engineering departments, but Quality is mostly the responsible function. When the auditor is performing the management review with top management, the question should be asked about the plan to reduce all nonconforming product. This is a requirement from the standard and it is usually found during the management review or in the record. If the auditor has missed this item, then review it again with the management representative. Ensure that there is a plan to reduce nonconforming product. This is money lost to the organization through scrap or bad processes. It behooves the firm to recover this lost money.

Read the procedure to reveal the authority to disposition nonconforming product. This is to be defined either in the procedure or work instruction or some other controlled document. When reviewing the forms, records, or some other documents for the disposition, verify that the particular person or function has disposed the product to the required process described in the procedure. There have been occurrences when the wrong entity has released product and a resulting customer complaint ensues. During the manufacturing audit, look for the proper identification of the nonconforming area(s) and on the product. The procedure is to describe what is the identification used. Also note who is to be notified when there is nonconforming product. The Quality Responsibility clause requires that person(s) with authority for corrective action are to be promptly informed. This is to be covered in this procedure. The key item to focus on in the review of the nonconforming records or documentation is the use of the term "use as is". The auditor is to verify that this disposition does not involve customer requirements as per the design record(drawing). There is to be a written approval for any deviation that is not to the current approval. The current approval is the Production Approval Process that was mentioned in the chapter on Engineering. The approval of out of specification material for shipment to the customer, any customer, is a major nonconformance. This aspect of the audit is very important to the auditor and auditee. Federal regulations and safety items may be involved. This could cost the auditee a great deal of money and also involve legal ramifications. Every audit should include the review of the nonconforming records and areas.

The rework of nonconforming product is by definition an action to bring the NC product into conformity to requirements. Any rework is to have instructions that are available to the particular personnel performing the tasks. These instructions can be very detailed or general in nature depending upon the required task. The auditor should judge whether each is appropriate. This requires much experience and should better be left to the auditee. However, there are situations when the instructions are too general or vague. The particular situation will have to be observed to make this decision. Repaired product by definition is the action to bring the nonconforming product into fitness for intended use. This is a very different definition from nonconforming product. Repaired product does not necessarily have to be conforming product. Again, there needs to be a notification to the customer for a concession waiver. This is to be specified in the contract. It is important for both auditee and auditor to understand the definitions of each rework and repair of product. All reworked product is to be re-inspected after the rework has been performed. If it is not readily apparent, then ask how it is done.

In the course of the audit of manufacturing, there will be probably be a use of statistical process control (spc). The auditor is to verify that the control charts are being used in the prescribed manner. The procedure on statistical techniques will describe how out of control and unstable conditions are to be recorded on the control charts. If during the course of the audit in the manufacturing area, a control chart shows these conditions, then the aforementioned procedure is to have the relevant actions for manufacturing and management personnel. This section of the standard is probably the hardest to implement in the manufacturing area. It is important to know who has had the proper training in the area of statistics. Often there is a lack of local control training for the immediate manufacturing personnel. This is most likely for use of statistical techniques with the use of computer software. The local personnel that are the closest to the affected process are not trained in how to respond to the computer's identification of unstable events. The personnel want to act, but lack the techniques to do so. This is a cause of management for not providing the proper training.

In conclusion, the Quality function/process is usually responsible for the above items that I have just described. As I have mentioned, this is due to the lack of commitment from upper management. The best quality department is no quality department. All affected functions are to participate to perform for quality.

XVI.
Customer Specifics

The use of ISO/TS-16949 along with customer specifics compares to QS-9000. The auditee is to send to the registrar all of the customer specifics that are required. This was noted in the beginning of the book. The objective of the registrar and the auditor is to audit to these specifics for conformance as well as the specification. There can be many customer requirements. There is not enough space or time to describe all of the requirements from all automotive customers. There are requirements from the Big 3 that have been published. The auditee as well as the auditor shall be knowledgeable in these requirements. No audit should be done without an examination of the customer specifics. This chapter will cover only a general overview of customer items that the auditor and auditee should take into account during the audit and implementation of a system.

Qualifications of auditors is of a high importance. Certain customers require that auditors for the auditee be compliant to ISO-10011, section 2. This is a very strict requirement for an auditee's local internal auditors. This requirement says that there is specific amount of experience in the automotive industry and education. Also there is a certain amount time that has to be spent in the Quality function. As has been mentioned above, these are very strict requirements for the auditee. There could be excellent auditors in the employ of the auditee, but they do not have the prescribed experience or education. This is a distinct disadvantage to the auditee.

Changes to the product or process require notification to the customer prior to the implementation of the change. The specification requires that the auditee obtain written approval from the customer. Almost all of the automotive customers have a specific deviation permit and procedure to follow. It is imperative that the auditee know all of requirements from all of their customers and the required deviation permits. There have been major nonconformances written when these particular protocols are not followed. It is a common misconception that if an auditee is design responsible, then they are able to make changes without notification to the respective customer. This can never be the case for any customer. A good philosophy to follow for any change, notify the customer's purchasing authority for confirmation, waiver, or required data for production part approval. This cannot be emphasized too strongly. Anyone that has worked in the automotive industry knows of horror stories that began through innocent changes.

The production approval process can differ greatly amongst the various OEM customers. If the auditee is supplying the "Big Three", then the required process for product approval is the AIAG's PPAP manual. However, there can be additional requirements from a particular division of one of these OEMs. It is the responsibility of the auditee to follow the "special" guidelines that are requested. The auditee is to fully explain to the auditor the guidelines that are request before the audit. During the surveillance audit cycle, it is the obligation of the auditee to inform the registrar and auditor of these "new" requirements. The auditor is to audit the customer specifics along with the specification's requirements. It is the basis of both of these items that many of the OEMs relate an equal footing between QS-9000 and ISO\TS-16949. Failure to inform, could result in a delayed audit or minor nonconformance. Additional requirements can be formal signoffs by a joint team of the OEM and the auditee. These signoffs are usually performed during a production trial runoff to see if all of the required equipment, personnel, and gauging operations are ready for full start production. This is sometimes known "run at rate". Involvement of the OEM and the auditee can vary based upon the level of risk of the product or process or the particular vehicle launch team.

Annual verification of all part numbers is a requirement of some OEMs as the responsibility of the auditee. This verification can take the form of a dimensional layout or full sample submission. Each customer will have their own requirements. The auditee should have a schedule of when particular part numbers are due and should reflect this requirement in the control plan. The testing of the verification of the physical or material or durability tests are to referenced in the customer's design record. The auditor should first review this record to see which tests are required by specification or other such communication to the auditee. This is a common source of miscommunication between customer and auditee. There have been occurrences when the customer has not successfully communicated these requirements to the auditee. As before, when in doubt, ask for clarification and read the customers supplier manual(if one exists). The auditor should look for the actual test reports and not a summary sheet stating all tests passed. Check the dates of the reports to see if there are current and the resulting numbers. Again, test reports have been seen to show the same numbers,exactly!!. This is not to say that the auditee has mislead the auditor, there could be a mix-up in the application of dates and filing.

There are various packaging manuals that describe the prescribed method of shipping to the customer. It is up to the auditor to verify that the auditee has fully complied with these specifications. In addition, the auditee is to have in their possession the correct manuals or documents that are required for shipments. This is a difficult part of the audit for the auditor. The auditee may not always have the required documentation and the customer may not specify what is required for shipment. This can be best resolved during the audit of product realization. The auditee should ask the customer what is the required packaging requirements during the planning stage for a new or changed product. A checklist for planning similar to the QS-9000 APQP checklists is a good method to use when the planning stage is in effect. In addition to this is the proper labeling of the packages. Never assume that the labels are the same as always. Use the checklists and ask questions.

Record retention for any customer can vary widely. The Big 3 use the requirements of QS-9000 as record retention times. The specification states the auditee will state what are the times. There are other customers that may require a longer time period for retention or nothing at all. In the areas of safety requirements on the customer's design record or the auditee's, pay special attention to the regulatory or government requirements. The auditee is to notify the auditor and registrar of these special retention times and records.

Communications with the customer cannot be emphasized enough. The auditee is to have the capabilities to communicate with the customer in the correct format and timing. This means that electronic data transfer is to be in place at the auditee's organization. The auditor should know from the initial receipt of the documentation whether the customer requires this type of communication. In the areas of customer satisfaction, the auditee is to provide the auditor with the latest performance reports from the customer. Many of the OEM customers have these reports on the Internet. It is the responsibility of the auditee to review these reports on a periodic basis for customer satisfaction. The auditor is to expect these reports for every audit.

The foregoing listed items are only a sample of what is usually required of an auditee dealing with automotive customers. This is not a wholly exclusive itemized list. The auditor should be aware that there are customers that may have other requirements. The auditor is to be alert when auditing to ask and inquire what are the specific requirements in certain situations that were outlined above.

XVII.
Epilogue

As stated in the Prologue, the purpose of this book was to enlighten and educate those who are attempting to obtain certification to ISO/TS-16949 or have already been certified. The author realizes that there are may methods to audit Quality Management Systems. This is only one method. There is a constant source of variation in every aspect of our lives that cause random outcomes from what is predicted. This is to be expected in any endeavor. The author expects much criticism for what is written and declared in this book. It is to be welcomed if it is constructive criticism that will benefit the particular audience using this book. Remembering what Chicago's mayor said after the 1968 Democratic convention, "What seeds do they plant?".

Bibliography References

Out of the Crisis, W. Edwards Deming. MIT Center of Advanced Engineering Study, Cambridge, Mass. 1992.

Collected Writings, Thomas Paine. Library of America, 1995.

The Republic, Plato, A. D. Lindsay, Every man's Library. Alfred A. Knopf. New York—Toronto, 1992.

QS-9000:1998, Third edition. Daimler-Chrysler, Ford Motor Co., and General Motors Corp.

ISO/TS-16949:1999-03-01, 2nd printing. International Organization for Standardization. Geneva, Switzerland. 1999.

Measurement System Analysis Manual, 2nd edition. February 1995: AIAG.

Statistical Process Manual. First Edition,1992. AIAG.

Potential Failure Modes and Effects Analysis Reference Manual. Third edition. AIAG

Production Part Approval Process. Third edition, 1999. AIAG

ANSI/ISO/ASQ Q9001:2000. American Society for Quality. 2000.

ANSI/ISO/ASQ Q9000-2000. American Society for Quality. 2000

ISO-9001:1994-07-01. International Organization for Standardization. Geneva, Switzerland. 1994.

Peace and may you Prosper

0-595-27312-2

Printed in the United Kingdom
by Lightning Source UK Ltd.
9596000001B